# TO INSPIRE AND DESIRE

David and Charles

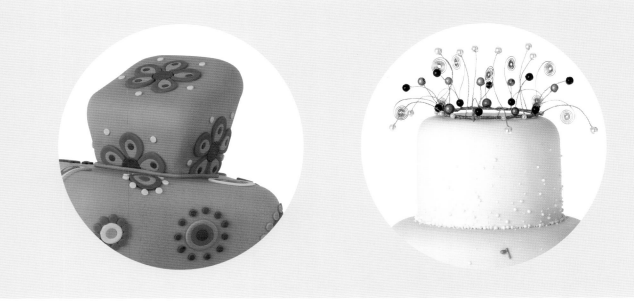

A catalogue record for this book is available from the
British Library.

ISBN-13: 978-0-7153-2497-4 paperback
ISBN-10: 0-7153-2497-7 paperback

Printed in China by Toppan Leefung Printing Limited
for David & Charles
Brunel House, Newton Abbot, Devon

Commissioning Editor Jennifer Fox-Proverbs
Desk Editor Bethany Dymond
Art Editor Sarah Underhill
Designer Emma Sandquest
Project Editor Jan Cutler
Production Controller Kelly Smith
Photographer Karl Adamson

David & Charles publish high quality books on a
wide range of subjects.
For more great book ideas visit: www.rubooks.co.uk

# contents

Introduction   4
Equipment List   6
Baking Cakes   8
Hints and Tips   12
Mini-cakes   13
Sugar Recipes   14
Covering Cakes and Boards   16
Carving and Covering Wonky Cakes   19
Stacking Cakes   22
Fascinating Colour   24
Cake Jewellery: The Basics   26

## Round Cakes

Ice-blue Jewels   30
Pastel Flower Tower   36
Art Nouveau Lilies   42
Perfect Harmony   50
Snowflake   58

## Square Cakes

Connoisseur's Delight   64
Funky Flowers   72
Greek Inspirations   78
Nursery Christening Bricks   84
Op Art Boxes   90

## Creative Cakes

Eastern Ornament   96
Falling Leaf   104
Sparkling Fish   112
Luxurious Orchid Wedding   118
Cosmic Christmas Ball   126

Templates   132
Acknowledgments   136
Suppliers   136
Index   137

# introduction

The title of the book says it all, as my aim with this, my fifth book with David & Charles, is to provide cakes that will indeed inspire you to be more creative and encourage you to try something new. For this book I have taken design themes that appeal to me, such as Op Art and traditional Indian patterns and, through the exciting process of research and design, I have created new and contemporary cakes for everyone to enjoy.

Apart from providing you with new ideas, the projects in this book are also very much in response to the many requests I have received from my readers at workshops, shows and via my website for written instructions for my most popular cakes. I love using cake jewellery on my cakes, as it adds that extra touch of sparkle and opulence, and from the feedback I have received it is obviously something that appeals to many others as well. I have therefore included a selection of jewellery-decorated cakes to inspire you. Experiment and see what you can achieve – I'm sure you'll be surprised at how simple it can be.

I have also let you into the 'secret' of how to create my extremely popular 'wonky cakes', a carved shape that I love using as it lends itself to all kinds of decorative possibilities. Once you've mastered the basics of this shape and feel more confident in your abilities, you can take the idea further (see my website for further inspirational ideas).

Be inspired, be creative, but most of all – enjoy!

*Lindy*

lindy@lindyscakes.co.uk
www.lindyscakes.co.uk

## about the book

The book is divided into three sections for the three types of cake – round, square and creative – and within those sections you will find a diverse selection of inspirational designs.

Most of the cakes in this book are made from several cakes, either stacked to create a large cake, such as Connoisseur's Delight, or to appear as a tiered cake such as Luxurious Orchid Wedding. The variations are endless and exciting, as you will see. There are also several versions of the much awaited and highly popular 'wonky cakes' with detailed instructions on how to achieve this free style. Full carving descriptions and templates for decorations mean that even those designs that seem the most complex are broken down into clearly explained stages.

Delicate jewellery decorates several cakes as crowns, bands or fountain-like toppers, and the book also describes how to develop the style even further for your own creations. Various decorative techniques are included, as well as a miscellany of effects you can achieve with cut-out shapes and textures. You can also create musical notes, champagne bubbles, realistic flowers and delicate mosaic.

If you like the idea of a large cake and want to transform it into a gift, each main cake is accompanied by equally as inspirational mini-cakes – many of them are like exquisite ornamented miniature boxes. You will also find suggestions for using some of the decorative elements from each cake to transform a shop-bought or plainly iced cake, as well as shortcuts for all the main cakes, giving you the opportunity to create something fantastic even if you are short of time or quite new to cake making and decorating.

Sparkling fish is a 'wonky cake' with a mosaic tier and wired topper.

## how to use this book

Please read the reference section at the front of the book thoroughly. It explains how to begin tackling the cakes as well as some basic techniques. The projects use a variety of implements, and the most frequently used are listed in the Equipment List on pages 6–7. Where particular makes of cutters or decorations are specified in the projects you will find an abbreviation for the name of the supplier in brackets. Please refer to the abbreviations list with Suppliers on page 136.

Recipes for the cakes, including baking times and quantities for various shapes, as well as all the different types of icing and sugar glue used in the book, are provided. To help you create the cakes, sketches and templates are provided at the back of the book.

For a professional look you will need to use paste colours and dusts. These can be obtained from cake-decorating stores or by mail order. Suppliers of equipment and ingredients can be found at the back of the book.

This square stacked cake, Op Art Boxes, is stylish and sophisticated.

Decorated with scrolls and piped decorations, the mini-cakes for Eastern Ornament make delightful gifts.

# preparation

If your cake is to be a creation that you will be proud of, you will need to be fully prepared. Before you start your chosen project read through the instructions carefully so that you understand what is involved and how much time to allow. Make sure you have all the material and items of equipment to hand that you will need to complete the project.

## time planning

Try not to leave everything to the last minute, and plan your decorating time in advance. As the cakes baked from the recipes in this book last about two weeks, you have about one week to decorate the cake, leaving a week for it to be eaten.
Each project is split into stages to indicate natural breaks in the decorating process; for example, a simple two-stage project, such as the Pastel Flower Tower, could be carved and decorated over a two-day period. Some projects are obviously more involved than others, for example Eastern Ornament and Falling Leaf, so try to be realistic with the time you have available, and plan well in advance.

# equipment list

**Cake boards:**
- Drum, a thick board to display cakes (1)
- Hardboard, a thin strong board used in the construction of stacked cakes (2)

**Cocktail stick** (toothpick), used as a marker and to transfer small amounts of paste colour (3)

**Cutters** come in various shapes and sizes for cutting out and embossing shapes (4)

**Dowels** are used to support cakes and make them stable (5)

**Foam pad** (PME), creates a surface on which to thin flower petals (6)

**Measuring spoons** for accurate measurement of ingredients (7)

**Moulds**, daisy centre stamps (JEM) used for creating flower centres (8)

**Multi-ribbon cutter** (FMM) is a time-saving tool for cutting strips of paste (9)

**Oasis fix**, a florist's adhesive for securing wires inside the posy pick (10)

**Paintbrushes**, a range of sizes is useful for stippling, painting and dusting (11)

**Paint palette** is used for mixing paste colours and dusts prior to painting (12)

**Palette knife** for cutting paste (13)

**Pins** (glass-headed dressmakers') to hold templates temporarily in position (14)

**Piping tubes** (tips) used for piping royal icing and cutting out small circles (15)

**Posy pick** for inserting onto cakes to hold wires (16)

**Reusable piping bag and coupler** to hold royal icing for piping (17)

**Rolling pin** for rolling out the different types of paste (18)

**Scissors** for cutting templates and trimming paste to shape (19)

**Set square** for accurate alignment (20)

**Smoother** helps create a smooth and even finish to sugarpaste (rolled fondant) (21)

**Spacers**, narrow and 5mm (³⁄₁₆in), for rolling out paste (22)

**Spirit level** to check dowels are vertical and tops of cakes horizontal (23)

**Stick embossers** (HP), small embosser used to add patterns to paste (24)

**Sugar shaper and discs** to create pieces of uniformly shaped modelling paste (25)

**Tins** (pans) (AS), small ball, multisized square and 5cm (2in) multiminis, for baking cakes (26)

**Tools:**
- Ball tool (FMM) gives even indentations in paste and softens the edges of petals (27)
- Dresden tool (FMM) to create marking on paste (28)
- Cutting wheel (PME) to use instead of a knife to avoid dragging the paste (29)
- Scriber (PME) for scribing around templates (30)
- Craft knife for intricate cutting tasks (31)
- Quilting tool (PME) for adding stitching lines (32)
- Fluting tool (JEM) for creating open centres in cut-out shapes (33)

**Work board**, non-stick, used for rolling out pastes (34)

## cup & US measurements

For readers who prefer to use cup measurements, please use the following conversions (note: 1 tbsp = 15ml; Australian tablespoons are 20ml):

**butter** 100g (3½oz) = 1 stick, 225g (8oz) = 1 cup, 25g (1oz) = 2 tbsp, 15g (½ oz) = 1 tbsp

**caster (superfine) sugar** 200g (7oz) = 1 cup, 25g (1oz) = 2 tbsp

**desiccated (dry unsweetened shredded)** 75g (3oz) = 1 cup, 4 tbsp = 25g (1oz)

**dried fruit**, 1 cup: currants 225g (8oz), raisins 150g (5oz), sultanas (golden raisins) 175g (6oz)

**flour** 150g (5oz) = 1 cup

**glacé (candied) cherries** 225g (8oz) = 1 cup

**icing (confectioners') sugar** 115g (4oz) = 1 cup

**liquid** 250ml/9fl oz = 1 cup, 125ml (4fl oz) = ½ cup

**nuts, chopped or ground** 115g (4oz) = 1 cup

**soft brown sugar** 115g (4oz) = 1 cup

## piping tubes

The following piping tubes have been used in the book. As tube numbers may vary with different suppliers, always check the tube diameter:

| Tube no. (PME) | Diameter |
| --- | --- |
| 0 | 0.5mm (0.020in) |
| 1 | 1mm (¹⁄₃₂in) |
| 1.5 | 1.2mm (¹⁄₃₂in) |
| 2 | 1.5mm (¹⁄₁₆in) |
| 3 | 2mm (³⁄₃₂in) |
| 4 | 3mm (³⁄₃₂in) |
| 16 | 5mm (³⁄₁₆in) |
| 17 | 6mm (¼in) |
| 18 | 7mm (³⁄₃₂in) |

# lining tins

Neatly lined tins (pans) will prevent the cake mixture from sticking and help to ensure a good shape.

## Straight-sided tins

1 Measure the circumference of your tin and cut a strip of baking parchment slightly longer than this measurement to allow for an overlap. Make the strip 5cm (2in) deeper than the height of the tin. Fold up 2.5cm (1in) along the bottom of the strip. For a round, or petal-shaped tin, cut this fold with diagonal cuts. For a square or hexagonal tin, crease the strip at intervals equal to the length of the inside edges of the tin, and then cut the folded section where it is creased into mitres (**A**).

2 Grease the tin and place the strip around the side(s) with the cut edge on the base. Cut a piece of baking parchment to fit the base.

## Ball tins

1 Care needs to be taken when lining ball tins. Cut two circles of the appropriate size from baking parchment:
15cm (6in) for a 10cm (4in) ball
20cm (8in) for a 13cm (5in) ball
25.5cm (10in) for a 15cm (6in) ball

2 Fold the circles into quarters to find their centres. Open out the circles and make radial cuts into the circle (**B**). Grease both the tin and one side of the paper and place the circle into the centre of one half of the tin, greased sides together. Encourage the paper to fit the tin by overlapping the sections.

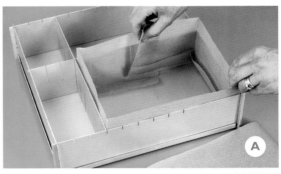

A

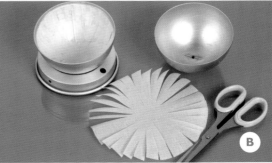

B

7

# baking cakes

## chocolate cake

This is a rich, moist, yet firm, chocolate cake. The secret to success is to use good-quality chocolate with a reasonably high cocoa solids content; for example, luxury plain Belgian chocolate with a cocoa solids content of around 50 per cent works well. See facing page for the recipe quantities.

1 Preheat the oven to 180°C/350°F/Gas 4. Grease and line the cake tin (pan) with baking parchment (see page 7).

2 Melt the chocolate, either in a heatproof bowl over a pan of simmering water or in a microwave. Cream the butter and sugar in a large mixing bowl until light, fluffy and pale.

3 Separate the eggs. Gradually add the egg yolks, then the melted chocolate to the creamed mixture. In a separate bowl, whisk the egg whites until they form soft peaks.

Gradually whisk the icing sugar into the egg whites.

4 Sift the flour into another bowl and, using a large metal spoon, fold the flour alternately with the egg whites into the chocolate and egg mixture.

5 Transfer the mixture into the lined bakeware, and bake. Baking times will depend on your oven, the cake tin used and the depth of the cake. Check small cakes after 30 minutes, medium-sized cakes after an hour, and large cakes after 2 hours. When the cake is baked it will be well risen, firm to the touch and a skewer inserted into the centre will come out clean.

6 Allow the cake to cool completely in the tin, then, leaving the lining paper on, wrap the cake in foil or place in an airtight container for at least 12 hours before cutting to allow the cake to settle.

## madeira cake

A firm, moist cake, Madeira will keep for up to two weeks. Allow one week to decorate it and one for it to be eaten. See facing page for the recipe quantities.

1 Preheat the oven to 160°C/ 325°F/Gas 3. Grease and line the cake tin (pan) with baking parchment (see page 7).

2 Cream the butter and sugar in a large mixing bowl until light, fluffy and pale. Sift the flours together in a separate bowl.

3 Beat the eggs into the creamed mixture, one at a time, following each with a spoonful of flour, to prevent the mixture curdling.

4 Sift the remaining flour into the creamed mixture and fold in carefully with a large metal spoon. Add the flavouring, if using.

5 Transfer to the lined bakeware and bake for the time given. Baking times will depend on your oven, the cake tin used and the depth of the cake. When the cake is ready it will be well risen, firm to the touch and a skewer inserted into the centre will come out clean.

6 Leave the cake to cool in the tin then, leaving the lining paper on, wrap the cake in foil or place in an airtight container for at least 12 hours before cutting, to allow the cake to settle.

*Carefully break each egg into a cup to prevent small pieces of eggshell falling into the batter.*

## flavourings

Traditionally, Madeira cake was flavoured with lemon, but it can also be made with other flavourings (flavourings are given for a six-egg quantity Madeira cake; increase or decrease the amounts for other quantities):

**Lemon** Grated rind of 2 lemons

**Vanilla** 5ml (1 tsp) vanilla extract

**Cherry** 350g (12oz) glacé (candied) cherries, halved

**Fruit** 350g (12oz) sultanas (golden raisins), currants, raisins or dates

**Coconut** 110g (3¾oz) desiccated (dry unsweetened shredded) coconut

**Almond** 5ml (1 tsp) almond extract and 45ml (3 tbsp) ground almonds

## using a ball tin: chocolate and madeira cakes

Bake sponge cake balls in two halves. Allow the halves to cool in the tin then level each cake using the edge of the tin (see levelling cakes page 16), and stick the two halves together with buttercream to create a perfect sphere.

Your cake can be made from one type of mixture or with sponge or fruit cakes for different layers.

# chocolate cake quantities

| Cake sizes | | | Plain (semisweet) chocolate | Unsalted (sweet) butter | Caster (superfine) sugar | Eggs (large) (US extra large) | Icing (confectioners') sugar | Self-raising (self-rising) flour | Baking times at 180°C/ 350°F/Gas 4 |
|---|---|---|---|---|---|---|---|---|---|
| 10cm (4in) round/ball | 7.5cm (3in) square | 7.5cm (3in) round x13cm (5in) deep | 75g (3oz) | 50g (2oz) | 40g (1½oz) | 2 | 15g (½oz) | 40g (1½oz) | 30–45 mins |
| 13cm (5in) round | 10cm (4in) square | | 125g (4½oz) | 75g (3oz) | 50g (2oz) | 3 | 20g (¾oz) | 75g (3oz) | 45 mins–1 hour |
| 15cm (6in) round | 13cm (5in) square/ball | 10cm (4in) cube | 175g (6oz) | 115g (4oz) | 75g (3oz) | 4 | 25g (1oz) | 115g (4oz) | 45 mins–1 hour |
| 18cm (7in) round/petal | 15cm (6in) square | | 225g (8oz) | 175g (6oz) | 115g (4oz) | 6 | 40g (1½oz) | 175g (6oz) | 1–1¼ hours |
| 20cm (8in) round | 18cm (7in) square | 15cm (6in) ball/ 15cm (6in) square x 10cm (4in) deep 15cm (6in) hexagonal (side to side) 23cm (9in) square x 4cm (1½in) deep | 275g (10oz) | 225g (8oz) | 150g (5oz) | 8 | 50g (2oz) | 225g (8oz) | 1–1¼ hours |
| 23cm (9in) round | 20cm (8in) square/18 x 23cm (7 x 9in) rectangular | | 425g (15oz) | 275g (10oz) | 175g (6oz) | 10 | 70g (2½oz) | 275g (10oz) | 1¼–1½ hours |
| 25.5cm (10in) round | 23cm (9in) square | | 500g (1lb 2oz) | 350g (12oz) | 225g (8oz) | 12 | 75g (3oz) | 350g (12oz) | 1½–1¾ hours |
| 28cm (11in) round | 25.5cm (10in) square | | 550g (1¼lb) | 450g (1lb) | 275g (10oz) | 16 | 115g (4oz) | 450g (1lb) | 1¾–2 hours |
| 30cm (12in) round | 28cm (11in) square | | 675g (1lb 7oz) | 550g (1¼lb) | 375g (13oz) | 20 | 125g (4½oz) | 550g (1 lb) | 2–2¼ hours |
| 33cm (13in) round | 30cm (12in) square/ hexagonal (side to side) | | 850g (1lb 14oz) | 675g (1lb 7oz) | 450g (1 lb) | 24 | 150g (5oz) | 675g (1lb 7oz) | 2¼–2 ½ hours |
| 35.5cm (14in) round/petal | 33cm (13in) square | | 1kg (2¼ lb) | 800g (1¾lb 12oz) | 500 (1lb 2oz) | 28 | 200g (7oz) | 800g (1¾lb) | 2½–2¾ hours |

# madeira cake quantities

| Cake sizes | | | Unsalted (sweet) butter | Caster (superfine) sugar | Self-raising (self-rising) flour | Plain (all-purpose) flour | Eggs (large) (US extra large) | Baking times at 160°C /325°F/ Gas 3 |
|---|---|---|---|---|---|---|---|---|
| 10cm (4in) round/ball | 7.5cm (3in) square | 7.5cm (3in) round × 13cm (5in) deep | 75g (3oz) | 75g (3oz) | 75g (3oz) | 40g (1½oz) | 1½ | 45 mins–1 hour |
| 13cm (5in) round | 10cm (4in) square | | 115g (4oz) | 115g (4oz) | 115g (4oz) | 50g (2oz) | 2 | 45 mins–1 hour |
| 15cm (6in) round | 13cm (5in) square/ball | 10cm (4in) cube | 175g (6oz) | 175g (6oz) | 175g (6oz) | 75g (3oz) | 3 | 1–1¼ hours |
| 18cm (7in) round/petal | 15cm (6in) square | | 225g (8oz) | 225g (8oz) | 225g (8oz) | 125g (4½oz) | 4 | 1–1¼ hours |
| 20cm (8in) round | 18cm (7in) square | 15cm (6in) ball/15cm (6in) square × 10cm (4in) deep 15cm (6in) hexagonal (side to side) 23cm (9in) square × 4cm (1½in) deep | 350g (12oz) | 350g (12oz) | 350g (12oz) | 175g (6oz) | 6 | 1¼–1½ hours |
| 23cm (9in) round | 20cm (8in) square 18 × 23cm (7 × 9in) rectangular | | 450g (1lb) | 450g (1lb) | 450g (1lb) | 225g (8oz) | 8 | 1½–1¾ hours |
| 25.5cm (10in) round | 23cm (9in) square | | 500g (1lb 2oz) | 500g (1lb 2oz) | 500g (1lb 2oz) | 250g (9oz) | 9 | 1½–1¾ hours |
| 28cm (11in) round | 25.5cm (10in) square | | 700g (1½lb) | 700g (1½lb) | 700g (1½lb) | 350g (12oz) | 12 | 1¾–2 hours |
| 30cm (12in) round | 28cm (11in) square | | 850g (1lb 14oz) | 850g (1lb 14oz) | 850g (1lb 14oz) | 425g (15oz) | 15 | 2–2¼ hours |
| 33cm (13in) round | 30cm (12in) square/hexagonal (side to side) | | 1kg (2¼lb) | 1kg (2¼lb) | 1kg (2¼lb) | 500g (1lb 2oz) | 18 | 2¼–2½ hours |
| 35.5cm (14in) round/petal | 33cm (13in) square | | 1.2kg (2lb 10oz) | 1.2kg (2lb 10oz) | 1.2kg (2lb 10oz) | 600g (1lb 5oz) | 21 | 2½–2¾ hours |

# fruit cake quantities

| | 10cm (4in) round/ball | 13cm (5in) round | 15cm (6in) round | 18cm (7in) round/petal | 20cm (8in) round | 23cm (9in) round |
|---|---|---|---|---|---|---|
| | 7.5cm (3in) square | 10cm (4in) square | 13cm (5in) square/ball | 15cm (6in) square/ hexagonal (side to side) | 18cm (7in) square/15cm × 20cm (6in × 8in) rectangular | 20cm (8in) square |
| | 7.5cm (3in) round × 13cm (5in) deep | | 10cm (4in) cube | | 15cm (6in) ball/ 15cm (6in) square × 10cm (4in) deep/23cm (9in) square × 4cm (1½in) deep | |
| Sultanas (golden raisins) | 50g (2oz) | 75g (3oz) | 115g (4oz) | 175g (6oz) | 225g (8oz) | 275g (10oz) |
| Currants | 50g (2oz) | 75g (3oz) | 115g (4oz) | 175g (6oz) | 225g (8oz) | 275g (10oz) |
| Raisins | 50g (2oz) | 75g (3oz) | 115g (4oz) | 175g (6oz) | 225g (8oz) | 275g (10oz) |
| Chopped peel | 25g (1oz) | 40g (1½oz) | 50g (2oz) | 75g (3oz) | 115g (4oz) | 150g (5oz) |
| Brandy | 7.5ml (1½ tsp) | 11.5ml (2¼ tsp) | 15ml (1 tbsp) | 25ml (1½ tbsp) | 30ml (2 tbsp) | 37.5ml (2½ tbsp) |
| Plain (all-purpose) flour | 50g (2oz) | 75g (3oz) | 115g (4oz) | 175g (6oz) | 225g (8oz) | 275g (10oz) |
| Ground almonds | 15g (½oz) | 20g (¾oz) | 25g (1oz) | 40g (1½oz) | 50g (2oz) | 70g (2½oz) |
| Mixed spice (apple pie) | 1.5ml (¼ tsp) | 2.5ml (½ tsp) | 2.5ml (½ tsp) | 3.5ml (¾ tsp) | 5ml (1 tsp) | 6.5ml (1¼ tsp) |
| Butter | 50g (2oz) | 75g (3oz) | 115g (4oz) | 175g (6oz) | 225g (8oz) | 275g (10oz) |
| Soft brown sugar | 50g (2oz) | 75g (3oz) | 115g (4oz) | 175g (6oz) | 225g (8oz) | 275g (10oz) |
| Eggs | 1 | 1½ | 2 | 3 | 4 | 5 |
| Black treacle (molasses) | 2.5ml (½ tsp) | 5ml (1 tsp) | 7.5ml (1½ tsp) | 15ml (1 tbsp) | 15ml (1 tbsp) | 20ml (4 tsp) |
| Vanilla extract | a few drops | 1.5ml (¼ tsp) | 1.5ml (¼ tsp) | 2.5ml (½ tsp) | 2.5ml (½ tsp) | 3.5ml (¾ tsp) |
| Glacé (candied) cherries | 25g (1oz) | 40g (1½oz) | 50g (2oz) | 75g (3oz) | 115g (4oz) | 150g (5oz) |
| Chopped almonds | 15g (½oz) | 20g (¾ oz) | 25g (1oz) | 40g (1½oz) | 50g (2oz) | 70g (2½oz) |
| Lemon rind and juice | ¼ | ⅓ | ½ | ¾ | 1 | 1¼ |
| Cooking Times (approx.) — 150°c/ 300°F/ Gas 2 | 30 mins | 30 mins | 50 mins | 1 hour | 1½ hours | 1¾ hours |
| Cooking Times (approx.) — 120°c/ 250°F/ Gas ½ | 30 mins | 1 hour | 1 hour 40 mins | 2¼ hours | 2½ hours | 3¼ hours |
| Total | 1 hour | 1½ hours | 2½ hours | 3¼ hours | 4 hours | 5 hours |

# fruit cake

1 Soak the sultanas, currants, raisins and chopped peel in brandy overnight.

2 Preheat the oven to 150°C/300°F/Gas 2. Sieve the flour, ground almonds and spice into a bowl. In another bowl cream the butter and sugar until light, fluffy and pale. Do not overbeat.

3 Lightly mix together the eggs, treacle and vanilla. Beat into the creamed mixture a little at a time adding a spoonful of flour after each addition.

4 Rinse the cherries and chop. Add to the fruit with the chopped almonds, lemon rind and juice, and a small amount of flour. Fold the remaining flour into the creamed mixture, followed by the dried fruit. Add extra brandy or milk if necessary.

5 Spoon into a lined cake tin (pan), level the top, and then slightly hollow the centre. Tie a double layer of brown paper or newspaper around the outside of the tin to protect the cake during cooking, and place a container of water in the oven to help keep your cake moist.

6 Bake for the stated cooking time and then reduce the temperature to 120°C/250°F/Gas ½ and bake further for the time suggested. For larger cakes cover the top with a double layer of baking parchment after 2 hours of cooking. When the cake is baked it will be firm to the touch and a skewer inserted into the centre will come out clean. Allow the cake to cool in the tin. You can add extra brandy to

| | 25.5cm (10in) round | 28cm (11in) round | 30cm (12in) round | 33cm (13in) round | 35.5cm (14in) round/petal |
|---|---|---|---|---|---|
| | 23cm (9in) square | 25.5cm (10in) square | 28cm (11in) square | 30cm (12in) square hexagonal (side to side) | 33cm (13in) square |
| | 350g (12oz) | 450g (1lb) | 550g (1¼lb) | 675g (1lb 7oz) | 800g (1¾lb) |
| | 350g (12oz) | 450g (1lb) | 550g (1¼lb) | 675g (1lb 7oz) | 800g (1¾lb) |
| | 350g (12oz) | 450g (1lb) | 550g (1¼lb) | 675g (1lb 7oz) | 800g (1¾lb) |
| | 175g (6oz) | 225g (8oz) | 275g (10oz) | 350g (12oz) | 400g (14oz) |
| | 45ml (3 tbsp) | 60ml (4 tbsp) | 75ml (5 tbsp) | 90ml (6 tbsp) | 105ml (7 tbsp) |
| | 350g (12oz) | 450g (1lb) | 550g (1¼lb) | 675g (1lb 7oz) | 800g (1¾lb) |
| | 75g (3oz) | 100g (3½oz) | 150g (5oz) | 175g (6oz) | 200g (7oz) |
| | 7.5ml (1½ tsp) | 10ml (2 tsp) | 12.5ml (2½ tsp) | 15ml (1 tbsp) | 17.5ml (3½ tsp) |
| | 350g (12oz) | 450g (1lb) | 550g (1¼lb) | 675g (1lb 7oz) | 800g (1¾ lb) |
| | 350g (12oz) | 450g (1lb) | 550g (1¼lb) | 675g (1lb 7oz) | 800g (1¾lb) |
| | 6 | 8 | 10 | 12 | 14 |
| | 25ml (1½ tbsp) | 30ml (2 tbsp) | 37.5ml (2½ tbsp) | 45ml (3 tbsp) | 52.5ml (3½ tbsp) |
| | 3.5ml (¾ tsp) | 5ml (1 tsp) | 6.5ml (1¼ tsp) | 7.5ml (1½ tsp) | 7.5ml (1½ tsp) |
| | 175g (6oz) | 225g (8oz) | 275g (10oz) | 350g (12oz) | 400g (14oz) |
| | 75g (3oz) | 100g (3½oz) | 150g (5oz) | 175g (6oz) | 200g (7oz) |
| | 1½ | 2 | 2½ | 3 | 3½ |
| | 2 hours | 2¼ hours | 2½ hours | 2¾ hours | 3 hours |
| | 4 hours | 4¾ hours | 5½ hours | 6¼ hours | 7 hours |
| | 6 hours | 7 hours | 8 hours | 9 hours | 10 hours |

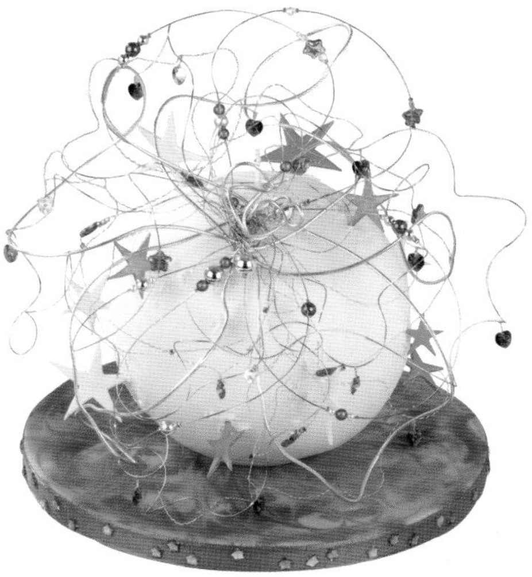

Using a ball tin is the perfect way to achieve the perfect sphere.

the cake while it is still cooling if you like. Prick the surface all over with a skewer and spoon some brandy over: 7.5ml (1½ tsp) for small cakes, 15ml (1 tbsp) for a 20cm (8in) cake increasing to 30ml (2 tbsp) for the larger cakes.

7 Leaving the lining paper on, wrap the cake in baking parchment and then foil. Never store your cake in foil only, as the acid in the fruit will attack the foil. Store the cake in a cool, dry place. Fruit cake should be aged for at least 1 month to allow the flavour to mature. Wedding cakes are traditionally stored for at least 3 months to give them a nicely matured flavour and to enable the cake to be cut cleanly into small portions. (Fruit cake that is not mature will be just as delicious, but difficult to cut neatly. Although fine for a family birthday, it would not be suitable for a wedding.)

# using a ball tin: fruit cake

Pile the mixture into the lower half of the tin, creating a dome, the height of which should be about 1–2cm (³/₈–¾in) from the top of the tin when it is assembled. This small space allows the mixture to rise and fill the tin while baking.

11

# hints and tips

Get the most of out your cake-making by adapting your favourite recipe or ensuring your cakes are just the right size by referring to the handy tips here. Also covered is a guide to the number of portions you can expect to cut from a cake.

## adapting a favourite recipe

If you have a favourite recipe that you would like to use for one of the cakes in the book then by referring to the chart on the right you can adapt it accordingly.

### how to use the chart

the chart assumes that your own basic recipe will be for a 20cm (8in) round cake, as this is the most common size. Therefore, if you want to make a 25.5cm (10in) round cake, for example, look at the chart and you will see that you need 1½ times the quantity of your usual recipe.

| Cake size | | | Multiples of your own basic recipe (approximate quantities) |
|---|---|---|---|
| Round and petal | Square and hexagon (measured side to side) | Ball | |
| 7.5cm (3in) | | | ⅛ (not really practical to make any smaller) |
| 10cm (4in) | 7.5cm (3in) | 10cm (4in) | ¼ |
| 13cm (5in) | 10cm (4in) | | ⅓ |
| 15cm (6in) | 13cm (5in) | 13cm (5in) | ½ |
| 18cm (7in) | 15cm (6in) | | ¾ |
| 20cm (8in) | 18cm (7in) | 15cm (6in) | 1 |
| 23cm (9in) | 20cm (8in) | | 1¼ |
| 25.5cm (10in) | 23cm (9in) | | 1½ |
| 28cm (11in) | 25.5cm (10in) | | 2 |
| 30cm (12in) | 28cm (11in) | | 2½ |
| 33cm (13in) | 30cm (12in) | | 3 |
| 35.5cm (14in) | 33cm (13in) | | 3½ |

## cake portions

The number of portions cut from a cake depends on whether the cake cuts cleanly and the dexterity of the person cutting the cake. The fruit cake portions on the chart have been based on 2.5cm (1in) square slices but many caterers do cut smaller than this, so your cake will go a lot further. However, it is always better to overestimate the number of portions required. Sponge cakes are served in larger portions, 5 × 2.5cm (2 × 1in), at least double the size of fruit cake slices. Allow extra cake if you want larger portions for, say, a teatime birthday cake.

| Cake size | | | Approximate portions | |
|---|---|---|---|---|
| | | | Fruit cake 2.5cm (1in) slices | Sponge cake 5 × 2.5cm (2 × 1in) slices |
| Round and petal | Square and hexagon (measured side to side) | Ball | | |
| 7.5cm (3in) | | | 9 | 4 |
| 10cm (4in) | 7.5cm (3in) | 10cm (4in) | 12 | 6 |
| 13cm (5in) | 10cm (4in) | | 16 | 8 |
| 15cm (6in) | 13cm (5in) | 13cm (5in) | 24 | 12 |
| 18cm (7in) | 15cm (6in) | | 34 | 17 |
| 20cm (8in) | 18cm (7in) | 15cm (6in) | 46 | 24 |
| 23cm (9in) | 20cm (8in) | | 58 | 28 |
| 25.5cm (10in) | 23cm (9in) | | 70 | 35 |
| 28cm (11in) | 25.5cm (10in) | | 95 | 47 |
| 30cm (12in) | 28cm (11in) | | 115 | 57 |
| 33cm (13in) | 30cm (12in) | | 137 | 68 |
| 35.5cm (14in) | 33cm (13in) | | 150 | 75 |

### tips for tiered cakes

It is very popular when making tiered cakes to provide different flavours for each tier so that there is something for everyone. However, you may need to adjust the sizes you bake slightly. For example, a finished covered fruit cake will be at least 1cm (⅜in) wider than, say, a chocolate cake of the same size, due to the additional layer of marzipan, whereas a Madeira will be about 1cm (⅜in) smaller than the chocolate, as the crust will have been removed from the cake. Therefore when baking a mixture of say fruit and Madeira, bake the Madeira cake a size larger and cut it down so that the balance between the tier sizes is maintained.

### tips for large cakes

■ Cooking times will depend on your oven as well as the cake tin used and the depth of the cake.
■ When baking a sponge cake, wrap paper around the outside of the tin (pan) as you would a fruit cake to prevent the edges of the cake becoming too dry. Once the crust is formed on the cake, protect from burning by either placing a paper or foil 'lid' over the cake or placing a baking tray on a shelf in the oven directly above the cake.
■ Check that your oven is large enough to bake the cake; for example an Aga or Rayburn will not bake anything larger than a 30cm (12in) cake, and some tins of even this size will not fit.

# mini-cakes

Capture the inspirational designs of the main cakes in this book to create perfect miniature versions. All of the main cakes have matching mini-cakes, which can be made to accompany the cake or as ideal gifts.

You can scale down the gorgeous designs to make miniature 'boxes' that are so lovely they are almost too good to eat. Let your inspiration flow with these easy-to-create little gems and make their designs as simple or decorative as you like. You can cut your mini-cakes individually from larger cakes or use special bakeware, such as a multimini cake tin that allows you to bake a number of small cakes at once.

*Scale down the designs from the mini-cake to create perfect miniature versions for greater impact.*

## baking mini-cakes using specially designed tins

- Choose a recipe for your mini-cakes – all the recipes in this book work well. If using the 5cm (2in) round multimini cake tin (pan) as used in this book, prepare the same quantity of batter as for an 18cm (7in) round cake.
- To prevent the cakes sticking to the tin it is best to line them. Otherwise, grease the tin well then sprinkle on some flour, and shake to cover all the greased surfaces. Remove the excess. Half-fill each section of the cake tin with the mixture and bake. The time required will depend very much on the type of cake and size of tin but, as a guide, 5cm (2in) round, sponge mini-cakes usually take 15–20 minutes.
- Leave the cakes to cool in the tin.
- Level the cakes by taking a large knife and carve across the top of each cake, using the edge of the tin as a guide.
- Mini cakes can dry out quickly so try not to leave them uncovered for any length of time.

Just by selecting one or two details from the main cake you can create a delightful mini-cake that would make a perfect gift.

# sugar recipes

Most of the sugar recipes used in the book for covering, modelling and decoration can easily be made at home. Use paste colours to colour them according to the individual project.

## sugarpaste

Ready-made sugarpaste (rolled fondant) is available from supermarkets and cake-decorating suppliers, in white and the whole colour spectrum. It is also easy and inexpensive to make your own.

**Ingredients** Makes 1kg (2¼lb)
60ml (4 tbsp) cold water
20ml (4 tsp/1 sachet) powdered gelatine
125ml (4fl oz) liquid glucose
15ml (1 tbsp) glycerine
1kg (2¼lb) icing (confectioners') sugar, sifted,
    plus extra for dusting

1 Place the water in a small bowl, sprinkle over the powdered gelatine and soak until spongy. Stand the bowl over a pan of hot but not boiling water and stir until the gelatine has dissolved. Add the glucose and glycerine, stirring until well blended and runny.

2 Put the sifted icing sugar in a large bowl. Make a well in the centre and slowly pour in the liquid ingredients, stirring constantly. Mix well. Turn out onto a surface dusted with icing sugar and knead until smooth, sprinkling with extra icing sugar if the paste becomes too sticky. The sugarpaste can be used immediately or tightly wrapped and stored in a plastic bag until required.

## modelling paste

This versatile paste keeps its shape well, dries harder than sugarpaste and is used throughout the book for adding detail to covered cakes. Although there are commercial pastes available, it is easy and a lot cheaper to make your own.

**Ingredients** Makes 225g (8oz)
225g (8oz) sugarpaste (rolled fondant)
5ml (1 tsp) gum tragacanth

Make a well in the sugarpaste and add the gum tragacanth. Knead in. Wrap in a plastic bag and allow the gum to work before use. You will begin to feel a difference in the paste after an hour or so, but it is best left overnight. The modelling paste should be firm but pliable with a slight elastic texture. Kneading the modelling paste makes it warm and easy to work with.

**Modelling-paste tips**

■ Gum tragacanth is a natural gum available from cake-decorating suppliers.
■ If time is short, use CMC instead of gum tragacanth. This is a synthetic product but it works almost immediately.
■ Placing your modelling paste in a microwave for a few seconds is an excellent way of warming it for use.
■ If you have previously added a large amount of colour to your paste and it is consequently too soft, an extra pinch or two of gum tragacanth will be necessary.
■ If your paste is crumbly or too hard to work, add a touch of white vegetable fat (shortening) and a little boiled water, and knead until softened.

## pastillage

This is a useful paste because, unlike modelling paste, it sets extremely hard and is not affected by moisture the way other pastes are. However, the paste crusts quickly and is brittle once dry. You can buy it in a powdered form, to which you add water, but it is easy to make yourself.

**Ingredients** Makes 350g (12oz)
1 egg white
300g (11oz) icing (confectioners') sugar, sifted
10ml (2 tsp) gum tragacanth

1 Put the egg white into a large mixing bowl. Gradually add icing sugar until the mixture combines together into a ball. Mix in the gum tragacanth, and then turn the paste out onto a work board and knead the pastillage well.

2 Incorporate the remaining icing sugar into the remainder of pastillage to give a stiff paste. Store pastillage in a polythene bag placed in an airtight container in a refrigerator for up to one month.

## sugar glue

Although commercially available, sugar glue is quick and easy to make at home. Break up pieces of white modelling paste into a small container and cover with boiling water. Stir until dissolved. This produces a thick, strong glue, which can be easily thinned by adding some more cooled boiled water. If a strong glue is required, use pastillage rather than modelling paste as the base (useful for delicate work, but not needed for any projects in this book).

## confectioners' glaze

Mix confectioners' glaze with edible lustre dusts to create metallic edible paint, such as used on the musical notes of Perfect Harmony. Confectioners' glaze is available from cake-decorating suppliers.

# buttercream

Used to sandwich cakes together or to coat them before covering with sugarpaste.

**Ingredients** Makes 1 quantity
110g (3¾oz) unsalted (sweet) butter
350g (12oz) icing (confectioners') sugar, sifted
15–30ml (1–2 tbsp) milk or water
a few drops of vanilla extract or alternative flavouring

1 Place the butter in a bowl and beat until light and fluffy. Sift the icing sugar into the bowl and continue to beat until the mixture changes colour. Add just enough milk or water to give the buttercream a firm but spreadable consistency.

2 Flavour by adding the vanilla or alternative flavouring, then store the buttercream in an airtight container until required.

## white buttercream

This is a useful alternative for those on a dairy-free diet. Simply follow the buttercream recipe but replace the butter with solid white vegetable fat (shortening).

## chocolate buttercream

To make chocolate buttercream, follow the buttercream recipe above and mix 30ml (2 tbsp) unsweetened cocoa powder with the milk or water before adding it to the butter and sugar mixture. Omit the flavourings.

## white chocolate buttercream

**Ingredients** Makes 1 quantity
115g (4oz) white chocolate
115g (4oz) unsalted (sweet) butter
225g (8oz) icing (confectioners') sugar, sifted

Melt the chocolate in a bowl over hot water and leave to cool slightly. Soften the butter and beat in the icing sugar, and then beat in the chocolate.

# white vegetable fat

This is a solid white vegetable fat (shortening) that is often known by a brand name: in the UK, Trex or White Flora; in South Africa, Holsum; in Australia, Copha; and in America, Crisco. These products are more or less interchangeable in cake making.

# royal icing

Use royal icing to pipe fine detail, such as on Eastern Ornament.

**Ingredients** Makes 1 quantity
1 egg white
250g (9oz) icing (confectioners') sugar, sifted

Put the egg white in a bowl and gradually beat in the icing sugar until the icing is glossy and forms soft peaks.

# flower paste

Available commercially from sugarcraft suppliers, flower paste (petal/gum paste) can be bought in white and a variety of colours. There are many varieties available so try a few to see which you prefer. Alternatively, it is possible to make your own, but it is a time-consuming process and you will need a heavy-duty mixer.

**Ingredients** Makes 500g (1lb 2oz)
500g (1lb 2oz) icing (confectioners') sugar
15ml (1 tbsp) gum tragacanth
25ml (1½ tbsp) cold water
10ml (2 tsp) powered gelatine
10ml (2 tsp) liquid glucose
15ml (1 tbsp) white vegetable fat (shortening)
1 medium egg white

1 Sieve the icing sugar and gum tragacanth into the greased mixing bowl of a heavy-duty mixer (the grease eases the strain on the machine).

2 Place the water in a small bowl, sprinkle over the gelatine and soak until spongy. Stand the bowl over a pan of hot but not boiling water and stir until the gelatine has dissolved. Add the glucose and white fat to the gelatine and continue heating until all the ingredients are melted and mixed.

3 Add the glucose mixture and egg white to the icing sugar. Beat very slowly until mixed – at this stage it will be a beige colour – then increase the speed to maximum until the paste becomes white and stringy.

4 Grease your hands and remove the paste from the bowl. Pull and stretch the paste several times, and then knead together. Place in a plastic bag and store in an airtight container. Leave the paste to mature for at least 12 hours.

**Using flower paste**

Flower paste dries quickly, so when using cut off only as much as you need and reseal the remainder. Work it well with your fingers – it should 'click' between your fingers when it is ready to use. If it is too hard and crumbly, add a little egg white and white vegetable fat – the fat slows down the drying process and the egg white makes it more pliable.

# Artista soft

This is used for the wired snowflakes. Artista soft is not an edible product but it is increasingly being used by cake decorators for decorations that do not touch the cake, as once it has dried it is lightweight and virtually unbreakable.

The paste, which contains no toxins or resins, is made from rice and potato flour plus a glue, so it sticks to itself and not your hands. It is soft and easy to handle and can be used for any type of modelling or moulding. Artista soft is available from an increasing number of cake-decorating suppliers (including Lindy's Cakes Ltd) plus arts, crafts and hobby suppliers.

# covering cakes and boards

Achieving the smoothest covering for your cake and board will give your cake a neat and professional appearance. With care and practice you will soon find that you have the perfect covering for decorating.

### levelling the cake

Making an accurate cake base is an important part of creating your masterpiece. There are two ways to do this, depending on the cake:

1 Place a set square up against the edge of the cake and, with a sharp knife, mark a line around the top of the cake at the required height: 7–7.5cm (2¾–3in) for the cakes in this book, unless otherwise stated. With a large, serrated knife cut around the marked line and across the cake to remove the domed crust.

2 Place a cake board into the base of the tin (pan) in which the cake was baked so that when the cake is placed on top, the outer edge of the cake will be level with the tin and the dome will protrude above. Take a long, sharp knife and cut the dome from the cake, keeping the knife against the tin. This will ensure the cake is completely level (**A**).

### filling cakes

It is not necessary to add fillings to the cake recipes used in this book. However, many people do like their sponge cakes filled with jam and/or buttercream. To add a filling, split the cake into a number of horizontal layers and add your choice of filling. The snowflake cake illustrates one buttercream layer (**B**).

### freezing cakes

Some of the cake projects in the book suggest the cakes be frozen. This allows you not only to bake the cakes in advance but also to carve them more easily without the cake crumbling and falling apart. How hard your cake freezes depends on the settings of your freezer, so it might be necessary to let your cake defrost slightly before attempting to carve it.

### apricot glaze

This glaze is traditionally used to stick marzipan to fruit cakes. You can also use other jams or jellies, such as apple jelly. Redcurrant jelly is delicious on chocolate cakes when a marzipan covering is used.

Put 115g (4oz) apricot jam and 30ml (2 tbsp) water into a pan. Heat gently until the jam has melted, and then boil rapidly for 30 seconds. Strain through a sieve if pieces of fruit are present. Use warm.

| Cake size | | | Marzipan quantities 5mm (³⁄₁₆in) thickness |
|---|---|---|---|
| Round and petal | Square and hexagon (measured side to side) | Ball | |
| 7.5cm (3in) | | | 275g (10oz) |
| 10cm (4in) | 7.5cm (3in) | 10cm (4in) | 350g (12oz) |
| 13cm (5in) | 10cm (4in) | | 425g (15oz) |
| 15cm (6in) | 13cm (5in) | 13cm (5in) | 500g (1lb 2oz) |
| 18cm (7in) | 15cm (6in) | | 750g (1lb 10oz) |
| 20cm (8in) | 18cm (7in) | 15cm (6in) | 900g (2lb) |
| 23cm (9in) | 20cm (8in) | | 1kg (2¼lb) |
| 25.5cm (10in) | 23cm (9in) | | 1.25kg (2¾lb) |
| 28cm (11in) | 25.5cm (10in) | | 1.5kg (3lb 5oz) |
| 30cm (12in) | 28cm (11in) | | 1.7kg (3¾lb) |
| 33cm (13in) | 30cm (12in) | | 2kg (4½lb) |
| 35.5cm (14in) | 33cm (13in) | | 2.25kg (4lb 15oz) |

**Note** These are the amounts of marzipan you will need to cover one cake. If you are covering more than one you will need less than the amounts for each cake added together as you will be able to reuse the trimmings.

## covering a cake with marzipan

A fruit cake should be covered with marzipan before the sugarpaste (rolled fondant) covering is applied, to add flavour, to seal in the moisture and to prevent the fruit in the cake staining the sugarpaste.

1 Unwrap the cake and roll over the top with a rolling pin to flatten it slightly. If the cake is to sit on a silver-covered cake board cover the top of the cake with a very thin layer of marzipan and then roll over this with a rolling pin (**C**). (The cake will be inverted, and this is to prevent the acid in the fruit dissolving the silver covering of the board – especially important if the cake is going to be kept for any length of time once covered.)

2 Turn the cake over so that the flatter surface (the base) becomes the top, and place on a piece of waxed paper.

3 Knead the marzipan so that it becomes supple; do not over-knead as this releases oils from the marzipan and changes its consistency.

4 Brush apricot glaze into the gap around the base of the cake. Roll a long sausage of marzipan and place it around the base of the cake (**D**). Press it under the cake with the help of a smoother, to fill any gaps (**E**).

5 Brush the cake with warm apricot glaze to help stick the marzipan and use small pieces of marzipan to fill any holes in the cake for an even surface. Roll out the marzipan between 5mm (³⁄₁₆in) spacers, using icing (confectioners') sugar or white vegetable fat (shortening) to stop it sticking to your work board or work surface. Turn the marzipan around while rolling to maintain an appropriate shape, but do not turn the marzipan over.

6 Lift up the marzipan over a rolling pin and place over the cake (**F**). Smooth the top of the cake with a smoother to remove any air bubbles, and then gently ease the marzipan down the sides of the cake into position, making sure there are no pleats. Smooth the top curved edge with the palm of your hand and the sides with a smoother.

7 Gradually press down with the smoother around the edge of the cake into the excess marzipan, and then trim this away to create a neat edge (**G**). It is best to allow the marzipan to harden in a warm, dry place for 24–48 hours to give a firmer base before decorating, although this is not essential.

### marzipan tips

■ Choose a white marzipan with a smooth texture and high almond content (at least 23.5 per cent).

■ Check you are not using icing (confectioners') sugar with added cornflour (cornstarch) to roll out your marzipan, as the presence of cornflour may cause fermentation.

## applying a sugarpaste covering

1 For a fruit cake, moisten the surface of the marzipan with clear spirit, such as gin or vodka. Form an even coating; if you leave dry patches, air bubbles may form under the sugarpaste (rolled fondant).

2 For a sponge cake, prepare the cake by covering it with a thin layer of buttercream to fill in any holes and help the sugarpaste stick to the surface of the cake.

3 Knead the sugarpaste until warm and pliable. Roll out on a surface lightly dusted with icing (confectioners') sugar, or if you have a large corian work board or work surface use white vegetable fat (shortening) instead. White fat works well, and you don't have the problems of icing sugar drying out or marking the sugarpaste. Roll the paste to a depth of 5mm (³⁄₁₆in). It is a good idea to use spacers for this, as they ensure an even thickness (**H**).

4 Lift the paste carefully over the top of the cake, supporting it with a rolling pin, and position it so that it covers the cake (**I**). Smooth the surface of the cake to remove any lumps and bumps using a smoother for the flat areas and a combination of smoother and the palm of your hand for the curved ones (**J**). Always make sure your hands are clean and dry with no traces of icing sugar before smoothing sugarpaste.

5 Take the smoother and, while pressing down, run the flat edge around the base of the cake to create a cutting line (**K**). Trim away the excess paste with a palette knife (**L**) to create a neat edge (**M**).

*If you find you have unwanted air bubbles under the icing, insert a clean glass-headed dressmakers' pin at an angle and press out the air.*

A pristine sugarpaste covering is essential for cakes such as this one that is simply decorated with jewellery.

## covering boards

Roll out the sugarpaste to a depth of 4mm (⅛in) or 5mm (³⁄₁₆in), ideally using spacers. Moisten the board with water or sugar glue. Lift up the paste and drape over the board.
Circle a smoother over the sugarpaste to achieve a smooth, flat finish to the board. Cut the paste flush with the sides of the board, taking care to keep the edge vertical. The covered board should then be left overnight to dry thoroughly.

Covering the cake board gives a cake that professional final touch.

*You can make your own spacers from strip wood available from DIY stores.*

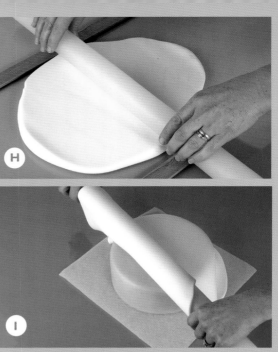

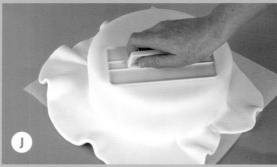

# carving and covering wonky cakes

Some of the most unusual cakes for weddings and other celebrations are stacked cakes cut at angles – the wonky cakes. They have a quirky appeal that lends itself to all kinds of decoration and can look particularly eye-catching.

Two methods to achieve this technique are listed below. Read through the section to see which one you would prefer to use.

*It is worth spending time getting the fundamental shape of these cakes correct – don't rush, especially if this is your first attempt.*

## baking the cakes

You have two alternatives when baking your cakes:

1 You can bake 7.5cm (3in) deep cakes and flip the top (as described below) to give the desired shape. This method is a little tricky.

2 Bake 10cm (4in) deep cakes or stack cakes to give the height (as described below). Although this is a more straightforward method it is also more wasteful as it creates more cake trimmings.

## carving the top slope

Level the cake to either 7.5cm (3in) or 10cm (4in) and carve as follows:

### 7.5cm (3in) deep cakes

1 Take four cocktail sticks and insert one into the top edge of the cake at 45 degrees (**A**). Insert the next opposite the first but positioning it horizontally on the side of the cake at a height from the base between 4cm (1½in) and 5cm (2in) – heights vary depending on the size of cake, please refer to the chart on page 20 (**B**).

2 Finally, insert the two remaining cocktail sticks at the midway points between the first two at the height indicated in the chart. You are aiming to create a cutting guide to help you carve away the top.

3 Take a long-bladed carving knife and, using the cocktail sticks to guide you, slice through the top of the cake (**C**). Leave the slice in place and position a cake board, the same size as the cake or larger, on top. Invert the whole cake, and then remove the main cake section from the top, placing it back on its base (**D**).

*Check that the sides are the same height at the same point and adjust as necessary.*

4 Spread buttercream (for a sponge cake) or boiled jam (for a fruit cake) over the sloping top of the main cake (**E**).

5 Carefully slide the top section from its board onto the prepared surface so that the two highest and two lowest sides match, thus giving the cake greater height and an increase in the angle of the slope (**F**).

**10cm (4in) deep cakes.**
Mark the cutting guide, as for the 7.5cm (3in) cake, but using the appropriate heights for the midway points. Take a long-bladed carving knife and, using the cocktail sticks to guide you, slice away the top of the cake to create a sloping top.

**freezing the cakes**
It is ideal, although not necessary if you are in a hurry, to freeze the cakes. It is much easier to carve and adjust the shape of wonky cakes when they are frozen.

# carving the sides of the base cake

1 Turn the base cake over, so that it rests on its top sloping side. Then, referring to the 'base diameter' column of the chart, take a round board of the correct size – that is, for a 25.5cm (10in) cake take a 20cm (8in) board – and place it in the centre of the base. With a knife make a shallow cut around the board to mark its position, so that if the board slips it is easier to replace in the same position. Next, carve from the edge of the board down to the outside edge of the cake – the surface that is resting on your work surface. Do this in small cuts to ensure you don't carve away too much cake (**G**).

2 Turn the cake back over, and straighten the cut of the sides if necessary. Also check that the cake is symmetrical, and adjust as required.

3 If using a sponge cake, take a small knife and carefully curve the top edge (**H**) to complete (**I**).

# carving the sides of the upper tiers

The only difference when carving the upper tiers of a wonky cake is that the board is not placed centrally on the base. The board needs to be nearer to the highest point of the cake to achieve the best effect; for example, for an 18cm (7in) cake the board should be positioned 1.5cm (⁹⁄₁₆in) from highest point and 3cm (1⅛in) from the lowest (see chart for placement)

*If your cakes are still partially frozen when you have finished carving, try stacking them, as for the finished cake, to check the side and slope angles, and so on. You can then adjust as required.*

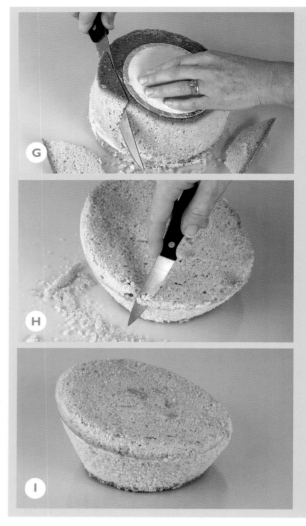

The wonky style is just right for an unusual cake using vibrant colours and bold patterns.

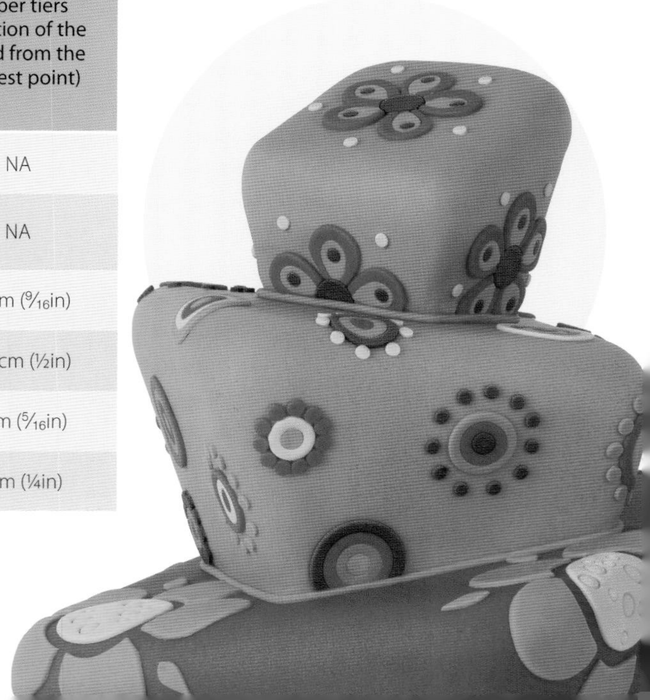

| Size of cake | Heights of sides | | | Base diameter | Upper tiers (position of the board from the highest point) |
| | Lowest point | Midway point | | | |
| | | 10cm (4in) deep cakes | 7.5cm (3in) deep cakes | | |
| 25.5cm (10in) | 4cm (1½in) | 7cm (2¾in) | 5.75cm (2¼in) | 20cm (8in) | NA |
| 20cm (8in) | 4.5cm (1¾in) | 7.25cm (2⅞in) | 6cm (2⅜in) | 15cm (6in) | NA |
| 18cm (7in) | 4.5cm (1¾in) | 7.25cm (2⅜in) | 6cm (2⅜in) | 13cm (5in) | 1.5cm (⁹⁄₁₆in) |
| 13cm (5in) | 5cm (2in) | 7.5cm (3in) | 6.25cm (2½in) | 10cm (4in) | 1.25cm (½in) |
| 10cm (4in) | 5cm (2in) | 7.5cm (3in) | 6.25cm (2⁷⁄₁₆in) | 7.5cm (3in) | 8mm (⁵⁄₁₆in) |
| 7.5cm (3in)* | 5cm (2in) | * | 6.25cm (2⁷⁄₁₆in) | 6cm (2⅜in) | 6mm (¼in) |

* 7.5cm (3in) cakes are not flipped.

## covering wonky cakes

Covering wonky cakes is very similar to standard round cakes. However, it is slightly more tricky as there is a lot more paste to be eased into shape.

*Cover the larger cakes first as these are easier.*

1 Roll out the sugarpaste to a thickness of 5mm (³⁄₁₆in) using spacers, and use to cover the cake (**J**). Carefully ease in the fullness of paste around the sides of the cake: start near the top of the sides and, using a cupped hand, stroke the paste in an upwards direction, gradually lowering your hand down the sides until all the paste is eased in (**K**). Be careful, as you don't want any pleats. If the paste seems to be forming a pleat, lift up the sugarpaste around the pleat to redistribute the paste and try again.

2 Smooth the sugarpaste, by firstly using a smoother to iron out any irregulars in the surface of the icing and then using the base of your hand to smooth and polish the top edge. Next, take the smoother and, while pressing down, run the flat edge around the base of the cake to create a cutting line (**L**). Cut away the excess paste with a palette knife.

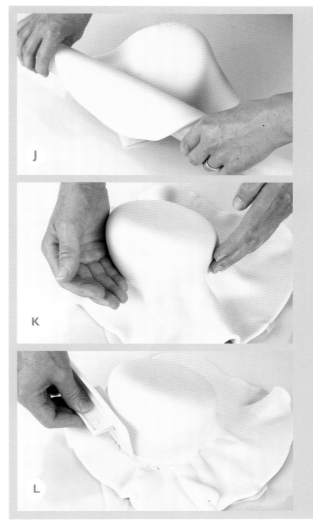

The relaxed form of this cake goes particularly well with the idea of fish peacefully swimming in a sunlit Mediterranean pool.

Decorated in softly muted pastel shades, this angled cake has a gently feminine appeal.

# stacking cakes

A multi-tiered cake needs a structure hidden within it to prevent it from collapsing. The following instructions take you through this important process. Separators add glamour and style to modern cakes and are available in several styles.

## dowelling cakes

All but the top cake will usually need dowelling to provide support.

**1** To dowel a cake, centre a cake board the same size as the tier above (or the size of the cake separator base plate, if dowelling is for a separator) and scribe around the edge of the board (**A**) to leave a visible outline.

**2** Insert a wooden dowel 2.5cm (1in) in from the scribed line vertically down through the cake to the cake board below. Make a knife scratch or pencil mark on the dowel to mark the exact height, and remove the dowel (**B**).

**3** Tape four dowels together. Then, using the mark on the inserted dowel, draw a pencil cutting line over the tape on the four dowels, making sure that the line is 90 degrees to the dowels (a set square helps) (**C**). Using a small saw, such as a mitre saw that holds the dowels firm as it cuts, saw across the dowels.

**4** Place one of the dowels back in the measuring hole and insert the other dowels vertically down to the cake board at 3, 6 and 9 o'clock to the first one (**D**).

**5** Repeat steps 1–4 for all but the top cake. **Note:** It is essential that all the dowels are inserted vertically and are all the same length, with flat tops.

### dowelling wonky cakes

The only difference here is that each dowel position will need to be measured and that the tops of the dowels will need to be cut at the same angle as the cake so that they will be flush with the icing.

## stacking cakes

### column cakes

These are dowelled and stacked before being covered with icing (see Art Nouveau Lilies, page 42). Cover the top of the each dowelled cake with buttercream (for a sponge cake) or apricot glaze (for a fruit cake) and a cake board or card for each layer. Then place the cakes directly on top of one another with a card between each layer, ensuring that their sides are vertical.

### tiered cakes

Each cake is covered with sugarpaste (rolled fondant) and dowelled before it is stacked (for example, Eastern Ornament). Place 5ml (1 tsp) royal icing within the scribed area of the base cake and stack the next-sized cake on top using the scribed line as a placement guide. Repeat the same process with the remaining cakes.

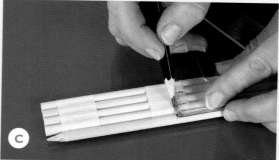

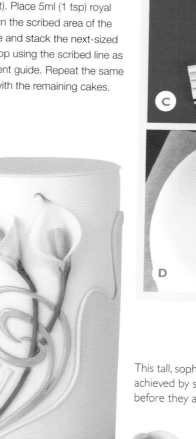

This tall, sophisticated effect is achieved by stacking the cakes before they are iced.

### using cake separators

Traditionally, pillars have been used to separate one tier from another. However, many other options are now available including elegant metalwork cake separators that add extra height and style to any cake.

1 Dowel the cake that the separator will rest on under the area of the base plate. Stick a thin cake card to the base of the separator using royal icing (**E**). (This acts as a barrier, as the separator should not come into contact with the cake.)

2 Position the cake separator on the dowelled cake using royal icing to secure. Leave the royal icing to set.

3 Once the icing has set, place a cake on the top plate and secure in place; for example, by using non-slip matting (**F**) or a little oasis fix.

An ornate, decorated separator extends Eastern Ornament grandly upwards.

# storage

Protect your cake by placing it in a clean, covered cake box, and store somewhere cool and dry, but never in a refrigerator. If the box is slightly larger than the cake and the cake is to be transported, use non-slip matting to prevent the cake moving.

**The following conditions will affect your decorated cake:**

- Sunlight will fade and alter the colours of icing, so always store in a dark place.
- Humidity can have a disastrous effect on modelling paste and pastillage decorations, causing the icing to become soft and to droop if free-standing. It can also cause dark colours to bleed into lighter colours and silver decorations, whether edible or not, to tarnish.
- Heat can melt icing, especially buttercream, and prevent the sugarpaste crusting over.

# fascinating colour

Probably the single most important aspect of decorating your cake is the colour you use to ice it, and getting this absolutely right is something that is well worth taking your time over. Colours are more than just decoration, though, as different colours create different moods. A little understanding about the amazing effects of colour will help you to develop your inspirational ideas.

## colouring paste

Brightly coloured sugarpaste (rolled fondant) and modelling paste in all kinds of colours are now available commercially. However, if you can't find the exact colour you're searching for, or if only a small amount of a colour is required, it is often best to colour your own paste or adjust the colour of a commercial one. The basic colour-mixing diagram below will give you a quick reference point for mixing paste colours.

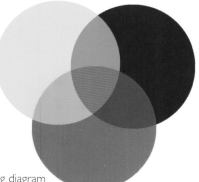

Colour mixing diagram

Depending on the amount of paste you wish to colour and the depth of colour required, place a little paste colour, not liquid colour, on the end of a cocktail stick (toothpick) or a larger amount on the end of a palette knife (**A**). Add the colour to the paste and knead in thoroughly, adding more until the desired result is achieved. Be careful with pale colours, as only a little colour is needed. Deep colours, on the other hand, require plenty and will become quite sticky. To overcome this, add a pinch of gum tragacanth and leave for an hour or two; the gum will make the paste firmer and easier to handle.

*It is easier to colour modelling paste when you are making it before the gum has taken effect.*

## colour symbolism

There are both positive and negative symbolic aspects associated with colours, which are familiar to each of us even though we may not be aware of them. This symbolism can be an important consideration when choosing a colour scheme. Below is a range of colours with some of their positive symbolic meanings.

| Red | Love, passion, excitement, strength |
|---|---|
| Yellow | Sunshine, springtime, youth, cheerfulness, wealth (gold) |
| Orange | Warmth, energy, happiness, vigour |
| Blue | Peace, calm, truth, sea, sky |
| Green | Nature, rest, tranquillity |
| Violet | Luxury, richness, royalty |
| Black | sophistication, smartness, drama |
| White | Bridal, truth, innocence, delicacy, honesty |

A striking sophistication is created by using black and white in the unique Op Art Boxes.

Bright orange is the perfect colour to express happiness and energy in Funky Flowers.

# painting cakes

You can paint over your cakes, and many fabulous effects can be achieved by painting dried sugarpaste. Painting also helps to brighten the overall appearance of a cake, as even vividly coloured paste will dry with a dull finish. Food colours behave in much the same way as ordinary water-based paints, so you can mix and blend them to produce many different tones and hues.

**Note** The coloured paste will appear slightly darker when dry. To paint sugarpaste, dilute some paste colour in clear spirit, such as gin or vodka. Using a paintbrush, a damp natural sponge or a stippling brush, apply to the dry sugarpaste. For deep colours, add a little clear spirit to some paste colour. For light colours, or if you want to apply a colour wash, add a little colour to some clear spirit. For details of flood-painting technique see Cosmic Christmas Ball, colouring the board, on page 129.

A stippling brush will give a subtle effect when used to paint sugarpaste.

*Allow yourself time to mix your colours as closely as possible to your chosen colour.*

For flood painting, colour is painted in large strokes then washed over with clear spirit.

Use a fine paintbrush to add intricate detail.

unpainted        painted

Painting adds depth of colour, as seen in Falling Leaf.

## lighting and its effect on colour

When deciding on your colour scheme, bear in mind the lighting that will be used when the cake is displayed, as lighting alters colours considerably. This is especially important for wedding cakes, which are set up in given positions.

**Candlelight** Many colours disappear, as the light is very weak. If a cake is to be displayed in candlelight, use tints; that is, small amounts of colour added to the white paste.

**Fluorescent light** This is disastrous with reds, which turn a muddy brown. However, blues are greatly enhanced.

**Tungsten lights** This lighting suits reds, oranges and yellow, but blues look dull and recessive.

**Good daylight** Generally the best light in which to display cakes, but daylight's effect on colour depends on which part of the world you live in.

Always try to use daylight to select and mix your colours to give the most accurate results.

# cake jewellery: the basics

Some of the most dramatic cakes in the book are decorated with toppers, crowns or garlands made of different weights and colours of wires and a variety of beads. The effects you can achieve are endless once you have some basic knowledge about the tools and equipment you will need.

## basic tools

You don't need many tools to be able to create effective cake jewellery:
■ Wire cutters (essential)
■ Jewellery pliers (essential)
■ Round-nose pliers (used to make coils)

## glue

You will need a strong acrylic-based non-toxic glue, available from most bead and jewellery-making suppliers.

## wires

It is very important that you use the right wire for the jewellery you wish to make. Some of the wires are interchangeable whereas others are not. The wires used in cake jewellery can easily be split into groups:

## soft beading/ binding wires

These are soft wires that are used in the creation of cake crowns and beaded garlands. They include the following:
■ Beading wire, 28 gauge is used in the book; others are also available (1).
■ Jewellery wire, 0.4mm (27g SWG/26g AWG), is slightly harder than the above but ideal if you want a true silver or gold finish. **Note:** Silver tends to tarnish (oxidise) once exposed to the air, so store your silver cake jewellery carefully. To prevent tarnishing over a long period of time, firstly wrap the jewellery in tissue paper, then place in an airtight bag and store in a dark, dry place.
■ Bullion wire. A crinkly wire, used in many crafts; here it is usually used to make beaded garlands (2).

## intermediate wires

These are stronger wires that can support a little weight; they are used to create cake fountains, wired cake toppers and elements of cake crowns, such as coils:
■ Jewellery/hobby wire, 0.6mm (23g SWG/ 22g AWG) (3), is ideal for coils and bead support on cake crowns. It is also thin enough to go through the holes in most

beads so it lends itself to beaded cake topper creations.
■ Metallic reel 0.5mm (0.020in) wire is similar to the above but manufactured for the floristry industry and available in a larger and more exciting colour range. This wire is fractionally stiffer to work with, although the size is not noticeably different (4).
■ Straight, paper-covered, floristry wire, available in many gauges with 24 gauge being the recommend strength for cake fountains. This wire is not suitable for cake crowns (5).

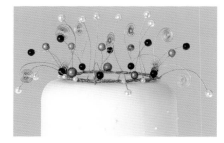

## strong wires

This heavy-duty wire is used for the base of cake crowns:
■ 1.2mm (18g SWG/17g AWG) jewellery wire. This is the wire that you bind all your cake crown elements to (6).

## aluminium wire

This is available in many widths, but for cake decorations the best ones to use are 1.5mm (16g or 17g SWG/52g AWG) and 2mm (14g SWG/12g AWG ). The wire can be easily bent to create any shape you wish; it is also available in an ever increasing range of colours, opening up many possibilities for cake decorators (7).

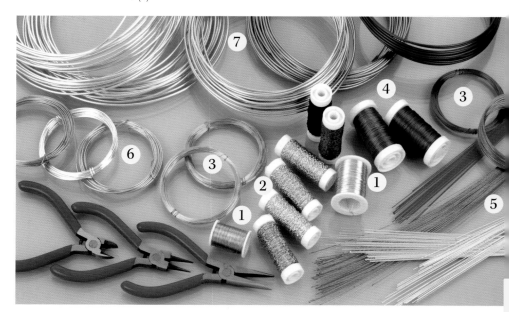

# beads

Beads can be used to complement a cake design, such as the Luxurious Orchid Wedding or be used with wires to create the only decoration; for example, Ice-blue Jewels.

There is a huge choice of beads available from around the world, ranging from cheap plastic to expensive crystal. Which beads you choose for your cake project will depend on your budget and the effect you are trying to create.

Delicate and colourful, wired-bead trims and crowns on cakes are becoming extremely popular with brides, who often base the design for their cake crown on their wedding tiara. But the decorations can also be the perfect finish for celebration cakes for all kinds of occasions. Your choice of colours and beads will create the mood: soft pastels and pearls make ideal decorations for a traditional style of wedding, whereas fiery reds and oranges would suit a birthday cake or as a leaving gift, or to celebrate an achievement. How you bend the wires will also change the appearance of the decoration.

| mm | SWG | AWG | Inches |
| --- | --- | --- | --- |
| 0.2mm | 36g | 32g | 0.0076 |
| 0.3mm | 31g | 29g | 0.0116 |
| 0.4mm | 27g | 26g | 0.0164 |
| 0.5mm | 25g | 24g | 0.0200 |
| 0.6mm | 23g | 22g | 0.0240 |
| 0.8mm | 21g | 20g | 0.0320 |
| 1mm | 19g | 18g | 0.0400 |
| 1.2mm | 18g | 17g | 0.0480 |
| 1.5mm | 16g/17g | 15g | 0.0600 |
| 2mm | 14g | 12g | 0.0800 |

SWG: standard wire gauge (as used in the UK)
AWG: American wire gauge

**Sizes** Beads range in size from the tiny seed beads to large beads designed to be worn as pendants. Those measuring 6mm (¼in) and 8mm (⁵/₁₆in) tend to be the most frequently used in cake jewellery, although smaller beads such as silver-lined Japanese rocailles are used to add sparkle, and larger beads such as 12mm (¹⁵/₃₂in) pearls are added to create focal points.

**Shapes** Most people think of beads as round, but of course they are available in a variety of shapes. Round beads are the most frequently used for cake jewellery, but heart, star and cut crystal shapes are often appropriate, too.

**A mix of colours** Cake jewellery is most effective when it reflects the other colours used on the cake, including the icing. So, for example, if a cake is covered with an ivory icing, it helps to have a few ivory pearls in the jewellery to bring the design together. Blending and contrasting colour schemes also work well.

**Selecting beads** It is a good idea to place the beads you have chosen for a project together on a small tray so that you can see what they look like together. This also enables you to add or remove beads or colours to achieve a balance between the colours and shapes that you are happy with.

# Be inspired...

# ice-blue jewels

Try this simple but sophisticated touch for a wedding cake. Pearls, beads and crystals are delicately threaded onto fine wires to create sparkling ornamental jewellery to encircle a cake and an elegant crown on the top – a popular choice for many modern brides. Wired beads make elegant decorations for all kinds of celebration cakes, as you can see on the pages of creative suggestions that follow the project. The cake is so simple to make you could aim for a stress-free wedding by partially making the ornaments in advance, leaving the simple icing and final stages until nearer to the great day.

# you will need...

## materials

- sugarpaste (rolled fondant): 800g (1¾lb) ice blue, 1.5kg (3lb 5oz) white
- icing (confectioners') sugar (optional)
- white vegetable fat (shortening)
- cakes: 20cm (8in), 13cm (5in) round (see pages 8–12)
- buttercream, or apricot glaze and marzipan (see pages 16–17)
- clear spirit, such as gin or vodka (if using fruit cake)
- ½ quantity of royal icing
- snowflake edible lustre dust

## equipment

- 5mm (³⁄₁₆in) spacers
- 28cm (11in) round cake drum (board)
- smoother
- palette knife
- round hardboard cake boards: 20cm (8in), 13cm (5in)
- waxed paper
- dowels
- reusable piping bag and adaptor
- piping tubes (tips) nos 16, 4, 2, 1
- sparkly white ribbon and non-toxic glue stick

## for the cake jewellery

- ice-blue 0.5mm (25 SWG/24 AWG) metallic reel wire
- 23cm (9in) non-stick rolling pin
- wire cutters
- ice-blue bullion wire
- thick pencil
- an assortment of beads and pearls; Lindy used: 50 × 4mm (⅛in), 5 × 6mm (¼in), 12 × 8mm (⁵⁄₁₆in), 8 × 12mm (¹⁵⁄₃₂in) ivory pearls

- 26 × 6mm (¼in) Swarovski light azure crystals
- 5g (⅛oz) pearlised pale green rocailles
- 25 × 6mm (¼in) matt mint glass pearls
- round-nosed pliers
- flat-nosed pliers
- strong acrylic glue
- strong 1.2mm (18 SWG/17 AWG) width silver-plated jewellery wire

# preparation

### covering the board

Using ice-blue sugarpaste, cover the cake drum and trim the edges (see page 16). Place to one side to dry.

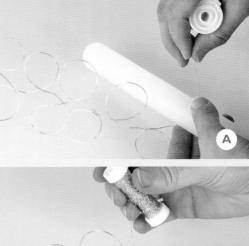

# stage one

### covering the cakes

1 Stick the cakes to their respective boards, using apricot glaze or buttercream, and then place on waxed paper.

2 Cover fruit cakes with apricot glaze and marzipan and then paint over the marzipan with clear spirit. For sponge cakes, cover with a thin layer of buttercream.

3 Use the white sugarpaste to cover each cake. Smooth the surface and trim away the excess paste (see page 18).

# stage two

### assembling the cakes

Dowel and stack the cakes (see page 22).

### piping pearls

Using the piping bag and no. 16 tube pipe a few royal icing pearls around the base of the top tier. With a no. 4 tube pipe a few more around the base. Continue, reducing the size of the tube, until the ring is complete.

*If your pearls are slightly pointed, quickly knock the point back into the pearl with a damp brush before the icing sets.*

# the jewellery

### making the loop-and-pearl decorated band

1 Take the ice-blue metallic reel wire and place the rolling pin on top of the wire about 5cm (2in) in from the end. Hold the wire in position on the pin with one hand while wrapping the reel end of the wire around the pin to form a circle. Reposition the pin on the wire, placing the wire on top of the pin. Hold in place and wrap the reel end around the pin to form another circle, to produce a very loose figure of eight.

2 Continue adding more loops to the wire until you have a length of about 80cm (31½in) (**A**). Your last loop should be on the opposite side of the wire to your first, so that the looped band will join up neatly.

3 Take the ice-blue bullion wire and a thick pencil, and make loops as before until you have an 80cm (31½in) length. Carefully place the two sets of loops together with the small loops on top. Loosely bind the loops together with bullion wire so that they lie flat (**B**).

### adding the beads

1 Thread a selection of your beads onto the ice-blue bullion wire. Hold the last bead threaded on the wire in one hand and the wire, either side of the bead, in the other and twist

the bead onto the wire by rotating it one-and-a-half times. Leave a 1–2cm (³⁄₈–³⁄₄in) space and repeat for the remaining beads on the wire to form a garland (**C**).

2 Take the beaded garland and loosely wrap it around the central section of the looped band (**D**) but do not cut off the excess.

## completing the band

Check that your band fits around your cake, then using the last section of the garland bind the two ends loosely together. Place the band over the stacked cakes so that it stands loosely against the side of the base cake.

## preparing the crown

1 Cut six 12.5cm (4⁷⁄₈in) lengths of ice-blue bullion wire. Thread beads onto a cut length in the following order: 4mm (¹⁄₈in) ivory pearl, 6mm (¹⁄₄in) mint pearl, pale green rocaille, light azure crystal, 4mm ivory pearl, 6mm (¹⁄₄in) mint pearl, pale green rocaille, light azure crystal.

2 Bring the beads to the centre of the wire then, using the thumb and index finger of one hand, hold the beads in place while you bring the wires together with the thumb and index finger of your other hand, so that the beads are locked into position. Twist the beads repeatedly while slowly allowing the wire in your other hand to slide through your fingers to obtain an even twist (**E**).

3 Twist the wire until the twist is 1cm (³⁄₈in) long then separate the wires to form a T shape. Make five more.

4 Cut six 10cm (4in) lengths of the ice-blue metallic reel wire. Take one and clasp one end of the wire between round-nosed pliers. Wrap the wire around one side of the pliers to create a perfect circle in the wire (**F**).

5 Place a dab of jewel glue on the wire next to the circle and thread on an 8mm (⁵⁄₁₆in) pearl (**G**) so that it rests on the glue. Leave to dry, repeat

for the five remaining wires. Once the glue has dried, measure 2.5cm (1in) from the end of each wire and bend the wire to create an L shape.

## assembling the crown

1 Cut a 30cm (12in) length of the strong jewellery wire and a few 30cm (12in) lengths of ice-blue bullion wire. Starting near one end, hold one of the prepared wire T shapes onto the strong wire and closely wrap the bullion wire around both wires on either side of the T to bind the two neatly together. Continue binding until you have a 2.5cm (1in) gap from the stem of the T, then place the L of the wired 8mm (⁵⁄₁₆in) pearl in position and bind until secure. Hold the next T so that its stem lies 2.5cm (1in) from the L already secured, then neatly bind to secure (**H**). Continue, alternately adding the T and L shapes every 2.5cm (1in).

2 To join the crown together, continue binding until you reach the end of the wire, then abut the two ends of the strong wire and continue binding, until you reach your start point. (Binding in the wire of the last L with the join ensures the ends of the strong wire stay together.)

3 Thread about eight 4mm (¹⁄₈in) ivory pearls and 25 pearlised pale green rocailles onto the bullion wire, varying the number of rocailles between each pearl. Hold the last bead threaded on the wire in one hand, and the wire, either side of the bead, in the other. Twist the bead onto the wire by rotating it one-and-a-half times. Leave a 5mm (³⁄₁₆in) space and repeat for the remaining beads. Make three more.

4 Take a garland and carefully wrap it tightly around the base of the crown so that the beads sit closely together (**I**). Add the remaining garlands. Cut away any excess.

5 Adjust the shape of the base of the crown to create a circle.

Using royal icing, pipe icing along the underside of the crown. Place the crown centrally on top of the top tier. Take a damp paintbrush and neaten any visible royal icing, then leave to dry.

## finishing touches

1 Paint over the iced pearls with some softened white fat, then, using a soft brush, carefully dust each pearl with snowflake lustre dust to add a shimmer. Attach the ribbon around the side of the board.

2 Once the royal icing holding the crown in place has set, position and bend the beads and wires as desired. **Note: remove the ornaments before carving the cake.**

# wired-bead inspirations

Create a more colourful, fresh and contemporary design to suit the occasion, with this beautiful collection of alternative beadwork designs. Try a variety of bead combinations and create movement in your decorations by bending the wires as seen in these examples .

## be creative

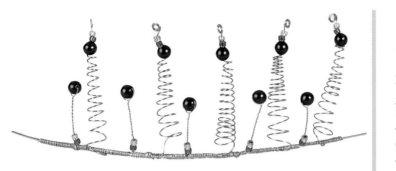

### spiral cones

To create spiral cones, make a small coil at the end of a length of wire, thread on two rocailles and then a 6mm (¼in) pearl. Holding the beads at the top of the wire, wind the wire carefully over a narrow cone, such as an acrylic glue pot. Finally bend an L shape in the end of the wire. To secure a bead in position on its stem, twist a bead onto some beading wire and continue twisting until the stem is of the length you require then bend the wire to form a T. Add the rocailles to the twisted pearl stems by threading them onto the twisted wire before creating the T.

**beads:**
• 6mm (¼in) royal blue pearls
• silver-lined rocailles, chocolate and gold

**wires:**
• 1.2mm (18g SWG/17g AWG) strong gold-plated wire
• 28 gauge gold beading wire/ 0.4mm (27g SWG/26g AWG) gold-plated jewellery wire
• 0.6mm (23g SWG/22g AWG) antique gold jewellery wire

## jewellery variations

The ice-blue decorations also look stunning made in green or pink.

### minty fresh

**beads:**
• 4mm (⅛in), 6mm (¼in), 8mm (⁵⁄₁₆in), 12mm (¹⁵⁄₃₂in) ivory pearls
• 6mm (¼in) emerald moon glass lamp bead

**wires:**
• mint bullion wire
• mint metallic reel wire

### pretty in pink

**beads:**
• 4mm (⅛in), 6mm (¼in), 8mm (⁵⁄₁₆in), 12mm (¹⁵⁄₃₂in) ivory pearls • 8mm (⁵⁄₁₆in) pink iridescent beads

**wires:**
• rose bullion wire
• rose metallic reel wire

## jewelled flower fountain

The crown here is placed around the base of the cake. **Note:** the diameter of the crown must be at least 1–2cm (³⁄₈–³⁄₄in) larger than the diameter of the cake once covered. See page 33 for instructions. (See page 123 to make the topper).

**beads:**
• 8mm (⁵⁄₁₆in) red wooden beads • 6mm (¼in) pearls, ivory, bronze and red • 4mm (⅛in) pearls, ivory and gold
• gold wire flowers with ruby glass centres

**wires:**
• 1.2mm (18g SWG/17g AWG) strong gold-plated wire
• 28 gauge gold beading wire/0.4mm (27g SWG/26g AWG) gold-plated jewellery wire • 24 gauge floristry wire (for the topper)

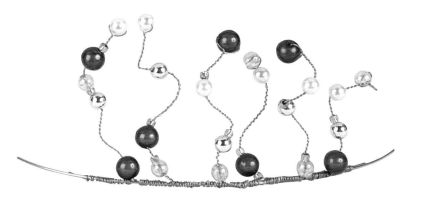

## waves and jewels

A simple one to create, twist a bead onto some beading wire and continue twisting until the stem is about 7cm (2¾in) long. Thread on a selection of beads then bend the wire to hold the beads at different points.

### beads:
• 6mm (¼in) pearls, ivory and silver • 8mm (⁵/₁₆in) cerise miracle beads • pink silver-lined rocailles • 6mm (¼in) pink iridescent

### wires:
• 1.2mm (18g SWG/17g AWG) strong gold-plated wire
• 28 gauge gold beading wire/ 0.4mm (27g SWG/26g AWG) gold-plated jewellery wire

## purple haze

Create the circle of beads as for the main cake and the coiled wire as described on page 54. Bend each completed wire stem to give movement.

### beads:
• 6mm (¼in) and 8mm (⁵/₁₆in) lilac iridescent beads • 4mm (⅛in) Swarovski crystals • pink and clear, silver-lined rocailles

### wires:
• 1.2mm (18g SWG/17g AWG) strong gold-plated wire • 28 gauge gold beading wire/0.4mm (27g SWG/26g AWG) gold-plated jewellery wire • 0.6mm (23g SWG/22g AWG) lilac jewellery wire/lilac metallic reel wire

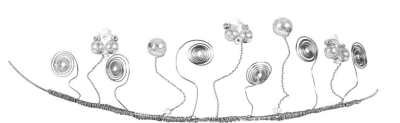

## floral gems

This decoration is created in a very similar way to the main cake but with the Ts placed at 1cm (³/₈in) intervals.

### beads:
• 6mm (¼in) red pearls • 8mm (⁵/₁₆in) deep purple • wooden beads
• silver-lined rocailles, red and purple
• 12mm (¹⁵/₃₂in) silver plastic crystal flowers (CB A-28)

### wires:
• 1.2mm (18g SWG/17g AWG) strong silver-plated wire • 28 gauge silver beading wire/0.4mm (27g SWG/26g AWG) silver-plated jewellery wire • 0.6mm (23g SWG/22g AWG) silver-plated jewellery wire/silver metallic reel wire

## crystal flowers

Create the flower and bead stems as for the main cake, then feed a flower and two bead stems through the centre of an 8mm (⁵/₁₆in) silver pearl. Make a T shape with the wires, making sure the bead stems are the same height. Then bind the T's onto the base wire at regular intervals.

### beads:
• 4mm (⅛in) silver pearls
• 6mm (¼in) plum and pink pearls • 8mm (⁵/₁₆in) silver pearls
• silver-lined rocailles, clear
• 22mm (⅞in) pink plastic crystal flowers (CB GM016)

### wires:
• 1.2mm (18g SWG/17g AWG) strong silver-plated wire
• 28 gauge silver beading wire/ 0.4mm (27g SWG/26g AWG) silver-plated jewellery wire
• 0.6mm (23g SWG/22g AWG) silver-plated jewellery wire/silver metallic reel wire

# pastel flower tower

Coral pink and lime green are the dominant colours used to create a softly feminine stacked, round cake in the wonky style. The combination of carved angled cakes, with the use of subdued pastel shades for the background and an array of contrasting cut-out flowers gives the cake a calm and relaxed appearance, ideal for someone who is gentle, peaceful and quietly confident. With its simple decoration and free form you can be as relaxed decorating it as the person who will receive it. Decorating using cut-outs is probably the simplest way to achieve an incredibly effective look, especially if the whole cake is covered with cut-out shapes. Find out more about creating the effect you want when using cut-outs by referring to the inspiration section on pages 40–41.

## you will need ...

### materials

- sugarpaste (rolled fondant): 1kg (2¼lb) coral pink, 600g (1lb 5oz) lime green, 1.1kg (2½lb) white

- cakes: 20cm (8in), 13cm (5in), 7.5cm (3in) round (see pages 8–12)

- icing (confectioners') sugar (optional)

- white vegetable fat (shortening)

- buttercream, or apricot glaze and marzipan (see pages 16–17)

- clear spirit, such as gin or vodka (if using fruit cakes)

- ¼ quantity of royal icing

- sugar glue (see page 14)

- modelling paste: 50g (2oz) each of three shades of pink, two shades of peach, lime green, and white, with a hint of coral.

*When mixing the pink and green colours, add a little coral so that all the colours tone with each other.*

### equipment

- 5mm (³⁄₁₆in) spacers

- 28cm (11in) round cake drum (board)

- smoother

- palette knife

- cake cards: 10cm (4in) round, 6cm (2³⁄₈in) round (cut a larger one down to size)

- waxed paper

- 15cm (6in) hardboard round cake board

- dowels

- sugar shaper with medium round disc

- fine paintbrush

- craft knife

- Dresden tool

- narrow spacers made from 1.5mm (⁹⁄₁₆in) thick card

- flower cutters: flat floral collection sets 1 and 2 (LC)

- piping tubes (tips) nos 18, 16 (PME)

- daisy centre stamp (JEM)

- pink ribbon and non-toxic glue stick

# preparation

### covering the board

Using coral sugarpaste, cover the cake drum and trim the edges (see page 16). Place to one side to dry.

# stage one

### carving the cakes

Carve the cakes following the instructions on pages 19–20. It is worth taking care to get the basic shape correct at this early stage to ensure a good balance to your cake.

### covering the cakes

1 Stick the 13cm (5in) cake onto the 10cm (4in) cake card, using apricot glaze or buttercream, and then place on waxed paper. If using a fruit cake, cover with apricot glaze and marzipan, then follow directions for sugarpaste below.

2 To help the sugarpaste stick to the cake, cover with a thin layer of buttercream (for a sponge cake) or paint over the marzipan with clear spirit (for a fruit cake).

3 Roll out the lime-green sugarpaste and use to cover the cake (see page 21) (**A**). Ease in the fullness of paste around the sides of the cake (**B**). If the paste seems to be forming a pleat, lift up the sugarpaste around the pleat to redistribute the paste, and try again.

4 Smooth the sugarpaste, and use the smoother to create a cutting line (see page 21) (**C**). Cut away the excess paste with a palette knife.

5 Knead a little of the coral pink sugarpaste trimmings into the white sugarpaste to give a warm hint to the paste.

6 Stick the 20cm (8in) round cake onto the 15cm (6in) cake board and place on waxed paper. Cover the cake with a thin layer of buttercream or paint clear spirit over the marzipan, as necessary. Cover the cake using the tinted white sugarpaste.

7 Stick the 7.5cm (3in) round cake onto the 6cm (2³⁄₈in) cake card and place on waxed paper. Cover with the remaining coral pink sugarpaste. Leave to dry.

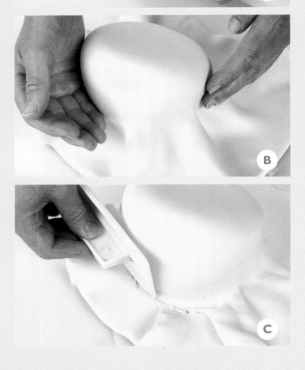

*Knead your modelling paste until it is the consistency of chewing gum.*

# stage two

### stacking the cakes

1 Remove the base tier from its waxed paper and place it centrally on the prepared cake drum. Dowel the base and second tiers (see page 22).

2 Using a small amount of royal icing attach the middle tier centrally on top of the base tier and the top tier on top of the middle, so that the high side of one tier corresponds with the shallow side of another (see main picture).

### adding trim

1 Soften some light peach modelling paste by kneading in some white vegetable fat and partially dunking the paste into boiled water. Knead again. Put in the sugar shaper with the medium round disc.

2 With a fine paintbrush paint a line of sugar glue around the base of the larger cake. Squeeze out a length of paste (**D**) and carefully place it around the base of the cake. Cut each end at 45 degrees using a craft knife so that the two ends will fit snugly. Glue the ends together and blend the join with the wide end of a Dresden tool.

pastel flower tower

38

# adding the flowers

## eight-petal light peach flower

**1** Knead some light peach modelling paste to warm it (add a little white fat and/or boiled water, if necessary, to soften). The paste should be firm but with some elasticity.

**2** Roll out between narrow spacers and cut out about 20 flowers using the eight-petal (rounded) flat floral cutter. To get a clean cut, place the paste over the cutter and roll over with a rolling pin (**E**). Run your finger over the edges of the cutter, then turn the cutter over and press out the paste.

*You may find a soft paintbrush useful to help ease the paste gently out of the cutter to avoid it becoming misshapen.*

**3** Knead some lime-green modelling paste and roll out between the narrow spacers. Use a no. 18 tube to cut out circles for the flower centres (**F**). Stick a circle onto the middle of each flower. Leave to partially harden, this makes them easier to pick up and handle.

**4** Paint some glue over the back of a partially dried flower and attach to the cake using the brush to help with placement. Arrange the remaining flowers randomly over the base tier and sides of the middle and top tier.

**5** Where the flowers on the sides of the cakes abut the trim on a tier, cut across one section of petals with a craft knife for a snug fit (**G**). Where the flowers on the base tier abut the middle tier, cut away a section of petals using a 10cm (4in) round board as a marker (**H**) to give a close fit.

## five-petal dark peach flowers

Create flowers as before using the dark peach modelling paste and the five-petal flat floral cutter. Create centres by rolling small balls of dark pink modelling paste, flattening them slightly once they are stuck in position.

## eight-petal mid-pink flowers

Create as before but cut out the centres from dark peach paste using the wider end of a piping tube.

## eight-petal dark pink flowers

Create as above. Make centres by pressing small balls of light peach modelling paste into a 1cm (³/₈in) daisy centre stamp (**I**). Paint some glue over the back of a partially dried flower and attach to the cake using the brush to help you (**J**).

## six-petal light pink flowers

Create as above but make the centres using the 7mm (⁹/₃₂in) daisy centre stamp and mid-pink paste.

## small blossoms

**1** Cut out a selection of small six-petal blossoms from lime green and white with a hint of coral modelling paste, using the smallest cutter in the flat floral collection. Create centres using a no. 16 tube.

**2** Attach the lime-green flowers to the base tier, the white with a hint of coral to the middle tier and both colours to the top tier.

## finishing touches

Attach the ribbon around the sides of the board.

# cut-out inspirations

Decorating using cut-outs is probably the simplest way to achieve an incredibly effective look, especially if the whole cake is covered with cut-out shapes. Apart from using different cutters to achieve variety, understanding how to get the most out of your colours for the background and cut-outs themselves is the key to a successful cake.

## the cutters

There is a vast range of sugarcraft cutters giving you a very effective and quick way to decorate your cakes. Cutters are usualy manufactured from plastic or metal, but which you choose very much depends on your own preferences and the shapes you are trying to create.

### plastic cutters

Usually manufactured in large quantities plastic cutters tend to be available in the basic shapes and sizes that most cake decorators require, such as hearts and simple flower shapes. They have the advantage over metal cutters in that they do not become misshapen with use; however, they have to be stored carefully as their cutting edges can become damaged by other tools and cutters. The quality of cutting edges also varies and they are often not as sharp as their fine metal equivalents.

### metal cutters

Although metal cutters are available in many more designs, the quality varies, so it's worth buying the best you can afford. You will find that they come in a variety of metal gauges: thinner gauges give a sharper cutting edge but become misshapen more easily, whereas the thicker gauges are more robust but tend not to cut as well. One of the advantages of choosing metal cutters is that they are often available in more intricate and delicate shapes than you would find in plastic.

## the cut-outs

Cut-outs are very simple to create, just use thinly rolled modelling paste and your choice of cutters:

### strong and pastel cut-outs

You can achieve two completely different effects simply by using strong or pastel tones. The cut-outs in the examples are the same but the effects they each produce is different. The pastel version gives a much softer feel than the stronger colours, which would be perfect for a more dramatic cake.

### dark colours

Because dark colours are recessive, they tend to disappear into the background. The yellow stars in this example seem to jump out at you whereas the blue triangle gives the illusion of a dark, triangular hole.

## different colourways: deep colours

The way you choose your colours will dramatically affect the appearance of your cake. This example shows three strong colours cut out in various colourways to illustrate the effects that can be created by using the same colours in different ways.

## simple shapes, great effects

You can create bold and pleasing effects using the simplest of cut-outs simply by your choice of colours. Try out some samples first before you decide on the overall decoration scheme to use on your cake.

## different colourways: pastel colours

The three pastel colours used in this example illustrate the effects you can achieve by using pastel colours in different arrangements.

## background colour

These squares use the same four colours in different orders, but the most striking difference is the background colour. Your choice of background colour will have a marked effect on the way the cut-outs appear themselves.

## simply spectacular

This amazing white wedding cake has an effective but simple floral cut-out layer and a dramatic topper to finish off (see page 123 to make the topper).

41

# art nouveau lilies

Elegant and beautiful, arum lilies were often used as motifs in Art Nouveau decoration, and today these sculptural blooms are becoming especially popular as bridal flowers. This smart and sophisticated column cake, made from round, stacked cakes, captures the beauty and simplicity of Art Nouveau design, with its soft curves and contrasting straight lines, combined here with realistic flowers made from flower paste. You can achieve the beautifully crafted lilies by using a simple template or cutter and delicately tinting the flowers with edible dusts. A perfectly elegant wedding cake, the design can also be scaled down to make exquisite mini-cakes to give as presents, below and page 49.

## Or make this cake for ...
• a leaving gift or special birthday cake
• anyone who appreciates elegance and sophistication • someone who loves lilies
• an engagement or anniversary – perfect because the lilies are in pairs.

43

# you will need...

## materials

- ¼ quantity of royal icing

- sugarpaste (rolled fondant): 700g (1½lb) cream, 1.4kg (3lb 1oz) white

- icing (confectioners') sugar (optional)

- white vegetable fat (shortening)

- sugar glue (page 14)

- modelling pastes: 75g (3oz) gold (colour to match edible gold dust), 50g (2oz) deep yellow, 450g (1lb) cream, 50g (2oz) white, 100g (3½oz) green

- semolina

- edible dust colours: deep yellow, brown, green, light-gold lustre dust (SK)

- cakes: three 13cm (5in) round (see pages 8–12)

- buttercream, or apricot glaze and marzipan (see pages 16–17)

- clear spirit, such as gin or vodka

- 100g (3½oz) white flower paste (petal/gum paste)

- confectioners' glaze

## equipment

- oval cake drums (boards): 30 × 25.5cm (12 × 10in), 25.5 × 20cm (10 × 8in)

- strong glue (optional)

- 5mm (³⁄₁₆in) spacers

- smoother

- palette knife

- straightedge

- embroidery embosser (PC)

- sugar shaper with medium and small round discs

- Dresden tool

- two 13cm (5in) round hardboard cake boards

- dowels

- waxed paper

- glass-headed dressmakers' pins

- scriber (optional)

- narrow spacers made from 1.5mm (¹⁄₁₆in) thick card

- craft knife

- small, sharp scissors

- cutting wheel

- large arum lily template or cutter (LC)

- medium arum lily template or cutter (LC)

- foam pad

- ball tool

- cocktail stick (toothpick)

- thin card

- selection of brushes, including a dusting brush

- cream velvet ribbons (in two widths) and non-toxic glue stick

# preparation

## covering the boards

Stick the smaller oval drum centrally to the larger drum using strong glue or royal icing. Knead the cream sugarpaste and roll out between 5mm (³/₁₆in) spacers using icing sugar or white vegetable fat. Place the paste over the smaller cake drum, bringing it over the edges. Smooth the top and top curved edge of the board then take the smoother and, while pressing down, run the flat edge around the base of the edge of the board to create a cutting line. Trim away the excess paste with a palette knife.

## adding the embossed border

1 Roll out 200g (7oz) of white sugarpaste into a long strip between the 5mm (³/₁₆in) spacers. Cut one edge straight. Position the smoother vertically against the cut edge of the paste, then place the embroidery embosser up against the

smoother and press it into the soft paste (**A**). Reposition and repeat along the straight edge.

2 Paint sugar glue over the uncovered surface of the larger oval drum. Place the embossed strip over the glue abutting the embossed edge to the cream-covered drum. Cut the paste to fit the board, and trim.

## adding trim

1 Soften some gold modelling paste. Do this by firstly kneading in some white vegetable fat to stop the paste getting sticky and then partially dunk the paste into a small container of boiled water before kneading again (the paste should have the consistency of chewing gum). Place the softened paste with the medium round disc into the sugar shaper.

2 Paint sugar glue along the join between the two cake drums. Squeeze out a length of paste from the sugar shape and place it over the

painted glue, cut to size and blend the join with the larger end of a Dresden tool.

## lily centres (spadices)

1 Roll the deep-yellow modelling paste into two 5.5cm (2¼in) long × 1cm (³/₈in) wide sausages and two 3.5cm (1³/₈in) long × 7mm (⁹/₃₂in) wide sausages. Place these spadices to one side.

2 Put some semolina in a small plastic bag and add some deep-yellow edible dust. Shake the bag to colour the semolina. Add more colour if necessary and shake again.

3 Cover a spadix with sugar glue, pop it into the bag of semolina and shake to cover (**B**). Remove and repeat for the other spadices. Set aside to dry.

# stage one

## preparing the cake

Level the cakes, and cut away the crusts if using Madeira.

**Sponge cakes** Place two cakes individually on the 13cm (5in) hardboard cake boards, securing in place with buttercream. Dowel the base cake and the middle cake (page 22). Spread a thin layer of buttercream over the top of each cake and stack into the required shape.

*You may wish to freeze the cake at this stage to make rolling it up in sugarpaste easier.*

Spread a thin layer of buttercream over the cake.

**Fruit cakes** Invert the cakes. Place two cakes individually on the 13cm (5in) hardboard cake boards, securing with apricot glaze. Dowel the base cake and the middle cake, and stack. Fill the spaces between the base and the layers with sausages of marzipan to create the column (see page 17). Cover with marzipan as described for the sugarpaste. Paint clear spirit over the marzipan.

## covering the cake

1 Knead the white sugarpaste to warm it, then roll out 100g (3½oz) into a circle between the 5mm (³/₁₆in) spacers. Place the circle of paste over the top of the cake. Place the smoother onto the surface of the sugarpaste so that it slightly overhangs the edge of the cake then, using a palette knife, remove the excess paste by cutting upwards against the smoother (**C**).

2 Roll out the remaining white sugarpaste into a long strip measuring at least 25.5cm (10in) wide. Turn the paste over and cut it into a 25.5cm (10in) wide × 50cm (20in) long rectangle.

3 Place the cake on its side onto the paste so that the covered top is flush with one long edge. Roll up the cake in the paste (**D**) and trim to create a neat, straight join. Rub the join closed. Trim away any excess paste from the base of the cake.

4 Stand the cake upright on waxed paper and leave to dry.

# stage two

## scribing the cake

1 Using a pencil, trace the pattern of the cake design on page 135 onto tracing or greaseproof paper. Cut the paper to the size of the template.

2 Place the prepared template around the cake so that the closed join in the sugarpaste is at the back of the design. Secure in place with a few pins then carefully scribe the pattern onto the cake by going over the pencil lines with a scriber or pin (**E**). Remove the pins and template.

## decorating the cake

1 Remove the cake from its waxed paper and place it close to one end of the prepared boards, so that the scribed pattern is facing forwards (see main picture).

2 Cut along the wavy line of the template to give you a template for the cream decoration on the cake. Roll out the cream modelling paste between the narrow spacers. Cut one long edge straight and place the template over the paste, aligning the cut edge. Leaving a margin of about 2.5cm (1in) between the template and your cutting line, cut around the template using a cutting wheel to give you a rough shape (**F**).

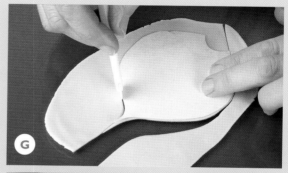

## attaching the cream decoration

1 Paint sugar glue under the curvy line on the cake, then carefully roll up the modelling paste and unroll it around the sides of the cake so that the paste overlaps the scribed line. Position the template on the cake, matching it up with the scribed line below the cream paste. Using a craft knife, cut around the edge of the template and remove.

2 Thinly roll out the white modelling paste and place it over the top of the cake to neaten the appearance. Cleanly cut the paste flush with the sides of the cake.

## adding vertical line and trim

1 Place some softened gold modelling paste inside the sugar shaper with the small round disc. Paint glue over the vertical scribed line on the cake. Squeeze out the paste over the glue. Trim to fit and use a straightedge to adjust if necessary.

2 Paint glue over the cut edge of the white modelling-paste disc. Replace the icing in the sugar shaper with softened white modelling paste and squeeze out a length over the glue. Cut to size and adjust the shape.

## the scrolls and decorations

1 Cut out the scroll sections from the original template with scissors. Roll out the gold modelling paste between the narrow spacers and place the scroll template on top. Using a cutting wheel, cut around each scroll section. Paint glue over the scribed scroll on the cake and position each cut section in place.

2 Cut out the shapes from the original template and cut these out from cream modelling paste. Attach as before.

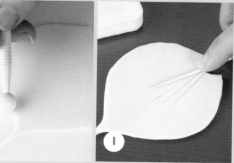

## creating the lilies

1 Make templates of the two lily spathes (page 134) if you are not using the cutters. Smear white fat over your work board, and then thinly roll out some white flower paste.

2 Place the larger template onto the paste and cut around the shape with a cutting wheel (**G**) or cut out the lilies with the cutter.

3 Place the paste onto the foam pad. Use the ball tool to stroke around the edges of the paste by pressing the tool half on the paste and half on the pad to soften the edge (**H**).

4 Press a cocktail stick repeatedly into the centre of the paste to create a radial pattern (**I**).

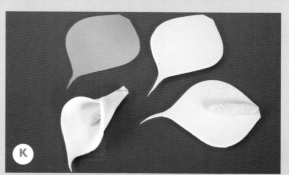

## assembling the lilies

**1** Take a large spadice and place it in position at the base of the spathe (see picture K).

Pick up the sides of the spathes and wrap them around the spadix, securing with sugar glue. Gently encourage the edges of the spathe to curl slightly outwards.

**2** Cut a 20cm (8in) circle from thin card and then cut in half. Form into a cone by finding the centre of the straight edge and wrapping the card around this point. Reduce the width of the cone until it matches the lily. Secure with tape.

Place the lily inside the cone to help it dry in shape. Use kitchen paper to stabilise the spadix (**J**). Repeat for the other large lily.

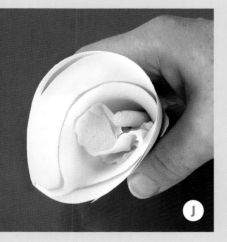

**3** Make two of the smaller lilies (**K**). This time place them directly in position on the cake using a little royal icing to secure. Leave to dry.

## dusting the lilies

**1** Using a soft brush, dust the centre of each lily with deep-yellow dust (**L**).

**2** On the larger lilies, dust the end tips of the spathe with brown.

Then dust with green just below the brown. Dust green onto the back of the spathes around and above the bases (see main picture).

## adding the large lilies to the board

**1** Knead, then roll, the green modelling paste into a long sausage 1cm (³/₈in) wide (you may find it easier to use a smoother). Cut the sausage into two.

Place one of the cut ends onto the base of a lily and, using a Dresden tool, blend the green paste of the stem up onto the flower to disguise the join.

**2** Attach the lily in position on the board, using a little royal icing, and wrap its green stem around the base of the cake. Cut the stem at 45 degrees at the back of the cake, then, using a paintbrush handle, hollow out the end of the stem.

**3** Add the stem to the second lily, and then position it close to the first with its stem resting on top of the first stem (**M**). Use kitchen paper to support the lily in position while the icing dries (**N**). Cut the stem of the lily so that it is just visible from the front of the cake, then hollow as before.

## gilding

Mix the light-gold lustre dust with confectioners' glaze and paint over the gold scroll and the trim (**O**) (wash your brush immediately afterwards).

## trim

Place some softened cream modelling paste in the sugar shaper with the medium round disc. Paint glue along the cut edge of the cream modelling paste added earlier. Squeeze out a length and position over the glue (**P**). Cut to fit.

*To get a true feel for the colouring of arum lilies have a look at the real thing.*

# stage three

### completing the small lilies

**1** Place some softened green modelling paste in the sugar shaper with the medium disc. Paint glue over the scribed stems on the cake. Squeeze out lengths of paste and place them over the glue. Cut the lengths where necessary to leave spaces (**Q**).

**2** Blend the stem into the flower with a Dresden tool. Mix some green dust with clear spirit and paint over the tip of each flower and the stem and back of the spathe (**R** and **S**).

### finishing touches

Using a non-toxic glue stick attach the ribbons around the sides of the large cake drum.

*If the paste doesn't come out of the sugar shaper easily or the shaper clicks, the paste is not soft enough. To soften the paste, first knead in some white vegetable fat to stop the paste getting sticky and then partially dunk the paste into a small container of boiled water before kneading again (the paste should have the consistency of chewing gum).*

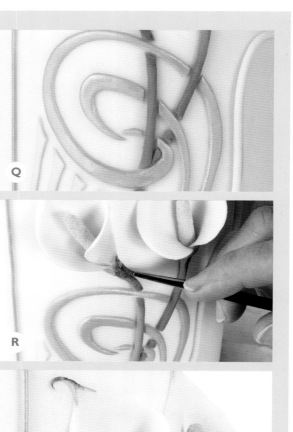

## love the look

• Make the delicate lilies to embellish any plain cake.
• An embosser is a quick and easy way to embellish the edges of a cake or board.
• Add the simple cut-out lines for a quick but smart decoration.

## simple shortcuts

• Make the simple column cake and place the lilies on top.
• Omit the decorative lines from the cake and just have the lilies curving up the side of the cake and around the base.
• Make the simple elements of the icing decoration but add fabric flowers to go up the side of the cake or bought icing flowers laid across the top of the cake.

## small wonders

**Capture the delicacy of the main cake to make these stylish mini-cakes that will make that extra-special gift.**

Bake your cakes in 5cm (2in) multimini cake pans or cut a larger cake into 5cm (2in) deep slices and then, using a 5cm (2in) circle cutter, cut the slices into rounds. Cover the cakes with ivory sugarpaste. Use the mini-cakes template on page 134 to make scaled-down versions of the lilies following the instructions for the main cake.

# perfect harmony

Tinted in creamy shades this simple round, stacked cake is transformed into an extravaganza to celebrate the success of a student or professional musician. A musical composition decorates the base tier, encircled by a garland of copper-wired beads. Piped champagne bubbles and musical symbols float up through the upper tiers, and the finale is a beaded cake crown. A music stave embosser makes the perfect staves for the base tier; notes and symbols are easily achievable using a tracing method.

Make the mini-cakes, see below and page 57, as gifts or to accompany the main cake.

### Or make this cake for …
• the wedding of a musical couple • a golden wedding, decorated with suitable romantic music • the birthday of someone who loves music – just make a single tier.

# you will need...

## materials

- 3kg (6lb 10oz) white sugarpaste (rolled fondant)
- paste colours:
  golden brown (Spectral – autumn leaf), chestnut brown (Spectral – chestnut)
- icing (confectioners') sugar
- white vegetable fat (shortening)
- cakes: 20cm (8in), 15cm (6in) and 10cm (4in) round (see pages 8–12)
- buttercream, or apricot glaze and marzipan (see pages 16–17)
- clear spirit, such as gin or vodka
- 1 quantity of royal icing
- antique gold (SK) edible dust colour
- 25g (1oz) dark brown modelling paste
- sugar glue (see page 14)
- confectioners' glaze

## equipment

- 5mm (³/₁₆in) spacers
- 28cm (11in) round cake drum (board)
- smoother
- palette knife
- stiff cardboard to make spacers
- musical stave embosser (PC)
- straightedge, such as a ruler
- set square
- cutting wheel
- round hardboard cake boards: 15cm (6in), 10cm (4in)
- piping bags
- piping tubes nos 0, 1, 1.5, 2, 3 and 4
- plastic film, such as the plastic envelope containing a greetings card
- sugar shaper
- paintbrushes
- dowels
- coffee ribbon and non-toxic glue stick

## for the garland and crown

- an assortment of beads; Lindy used:
  35 × 4mm (¹/₈in) and 15 × 6mm (¼in) ivory pearls
  40 × 6mm (¼in) rich-brown wooden beads
  40 × chocolate silver-lined rocailles
  35 × 6mm (¼in) burnt-orange miracle beads
  20 × 6mm (¼in) and 10 × 8mm (⁵/₁₆in) amber miracle beads
- copper bullion wire
- 4mm (¹/₈in) width copper jewellery wire/28 gauge beading wire
- 6mm (¼in) width antique gold jewellery/hobby wire
- strong 1mm (19g SWG/18g AWG) width copper jewellery wire
- wire cutters
- round-nosed pliers
- flat-nosed pliers

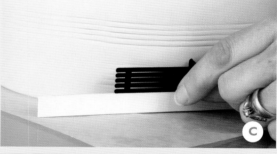

# preparation

## colour samples

**1** Make small colour samples. Take some white sugarpaste and add a little of the suggested paste colours to create a browny-cream colour for the cake board. Break off a small piece, roll into a ball and place to one side.

**2** Gradually add small amounts of white to the base colour to create lighter shades – you will need three additional shades. Ensure the shades look evenly balanced then roll one small ball of each and place to one side with the base colour (**A**).

## covering the board

Colour 1.4kg (3lb 1oz) of sugarpaste a browny cream to match your darkest colour sample. Roll it out between 5mm (³/₁₆in) spacers using icing sugar or white vegetable fat to prevent sticking. Lift up the paste and place it over the board. Use a smoother to smooth the paste level. Trim the edges flush with the sides of the board using a palette knife. Place to one side to dry.

## making spacers

Take the stiff cardboard and cut into two strips, one with a width of 1.2cm (¹⁵/₃₂in) and the other 4cm (1½in) – these will be used to help mark the music staves.

# stage one

## covering the base tier

**1** Place the 20cm (8in) cake on waxed paper and cover with buttercream or apricot glaze and marzipan. Take 450–500g (1lb–1lb 2oz) of the board sugarpaste trimmings and add enough white sugarpaste to make your second darkest shade.

**2** Roll the paste out and use to cover the cake. Ease in the fullness of paste around the sides of the cake and smooth using a smoother and the base of your hand. Use the smoother to create a cutting line around the base of the cake and cut away the excess paste with a palette knife.

## embossing the staves

**1** Place the 4cm (1½in) wide spacer onto the side of the cake. Take the stave embosser, position one long edge along the top of the spacer, and gently rock it around the side of the cake so that the lines are embossed into the soft paste (**B**). Remove the embosser and spacer, and reposition so that the lines join up smoothly with the first set. Repeat. Continue until the embossed stave encircles the cake.

**2** Next, place the 1.2cm (¹⁵/₃₂in) spacer up against the side of the cake and emboss the bass stave as for the treble stave just completed (**C**). If some of the embossed lines on the stave look a little faint, use a straightedge to touch up where necessary.

**3** Emboss the bar lines by placing a set square up against the side of the cake and running a cutting wheel along the vertical edge between the two outer lines of the two staves (**D**). Repeat at intervals – these do not need to be spaced evenly.

## the remaining tiers

**1** Place the remaining cakes individually on waxed paper with their respective hardboard cake boards beneath each. Cover with buttercream or apricot glaze and marzipan. Paint over the marzipan with clear spirit.

**2** For the middle tier take about 350–400g (12 – 14oz) of sugarpaste trimmings from the base tier and add enough white sugarpaste to make the correct shade. Then roll the paste out and use to cover the 15cm (6in) cake. Smooth and trim as for the base. For the top tier, colour the sugarpaste using the trimmings from the middle tier and white sugarpaste to make the correct shade. Then cover the top tier. Leave to dry.

## notes and notation

**1** Copy the music and music notation from page 133 or compose your own piece and enlarge it to fit the embossed staves. Free music writing programme downloads are available on the Web; the programmes are generally easy to use and prevent you making glaring errors in your composition. You can also listen to your piece being played.

**2** Colour about 50g (2oz) royal icing golden brown using a little of the paste colours, try to match the colour to the edible gold dust you will be using. Check the consistency of the icing and adjust it, if necessary, by adding either icing sugar or boiled water. Take two piping bags, snip off their ends and place a no. 0 tube in one and a no. 1.5 in the other. Half-fill with the coloured icing. Place a sheet of plastic film over the music.

**3** Position the no. 0 tube at one end of a note's stem, then gently squeeze and lift the tube away from the note allowing the icing to fall in position along the stem (**E**). Pipe a few more stems.

**4** To pipe a note, place the no. 1.5 tube on the end of a stem and gradually squeeze out icing to fill the note while moving the tube across the note (**F**). Repeat, adding notes to all the piped stems. When the notes are either minims or semibreves (the hollow notes) pipe around the outside of the note in one continuous movement.

**5** Join the quavers (the joined notes) together by piping the joining line with a no. 1.5 tube. Continue piping the notes until you have enough to fill the bars (the vertical lines) on your cake, plus extras to allow for breakages. Leave to dry thoroughly. For the second tier, pressure pipe over the musical notation in the same manner, using appropriate tube sizes. Pipe two or three sets of these. Leave to dry.

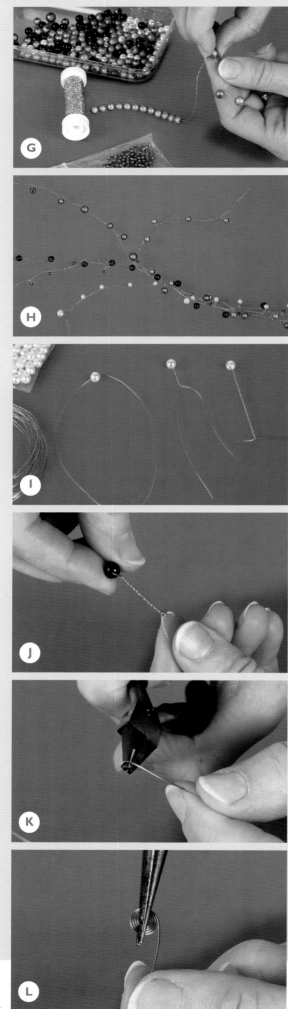

## making the garlands

1 Select one type of bead and thread approximately 30 – 35 onto the copper bullion wire. Hold the last threaded bead in one hand, and the wire, either side of the bead, in the other and twist the bead onto the wire by rotating it one-and-a-half times. Leave a space, and repeat for the remaining beads on the wire (**G**). Check that the garland is long enough to go around the base of the cake then twist the wire ends into the garland so that a bead sits at either end.

2 Create individual garlands for the other types of beads you have chosen (**H**). Arrange the garlands loosely around the base of the cake, interweaving the ends of each so that they are secure.

## preparing the crown

1 Cut ten 15cm (6in) lengths of the copper beading wire. Take a 6mm (¼in) ivory pearl and thread it onto of the cut lengths. Using your thumb and index finger of one hand, hold the pearl in the middle of the wire then bring the wires together between your thumb and index finger of your other hand so that the pearl is locked into position. Twist the pearl repeatedly while slowly allowing the wire in your other hand to slide through your fingers to obtain an even twist (see picture I).

2 Twist the wire until the twist is 5cm (2in) long, then separate the wires to form a T-shape (**I**). Make nine more.

3 Take five burnt-orange miracle beads and twist them individually onto the copper wire, creating a twist

length of 2.3cm (¹⁵⁄₁₆in). Create the T-shape in the wire as above.

4 Take five rich-brown wooden beads and twist them individually onto the copper wire creating a twist length of 3.5cm (1³⁄₈in) (**J**), then thread an amber miracle bead onto each twist before creating the T-shape in the wire.

5 For the coils, cut approximately 25cm (9⅞in) of antique gold jewellery wire, clasp one end of the wire between round-nosed pliers and wrap the wire around one side of the pliers to create a perfect circle in the wire (**K**). Place the circle horizontally between a pair of flat-nosed pliers and, with your spare hand, push the wire away from you so that it wraps itself partly around the central circle. Reposition the circle and wrap more wire around the circle; you are aiming to wrap about a quarter of the circle before repositioning it (**L**). Repeat until the circle is large enough to hold in your fingers, then, using your fingers, continue coiling the wire until the coil has a diameter of 1.3cm (½in). Measure 3cm (1⅛in) from the coil and bend the wire to create an L-shape. Repeat to make ten coils in total.

6 Thread two coil stems and the twist of an amber miracle bead (undo the T-shape) through the hole of a rich-brown wooden bead, then reposition the wires to create the required T-shape as seen in the picture (**M**). Repeat to make five groupings.

7 Take ten 4mm (¹⁄₈in) ivory pearls and twist them onto short lengths of copper bullion wire then cut each twist to a length of 1.5cm (⁹⁄₁₆in).

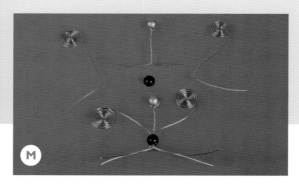

# stage two

## assembling the crown

**1** Cut a 24cm (9½in) length of the strong jewellery wire and a few 30cm (12in) lengths of copper beading wire. Starting near one end, hold one of the prepared wire T-shapes onto the strong wire and wrap the beading wire around both wires on one side of the T to bind the two neatly together. Hold the next T so that its twist lies 1cm (³/₈in) from the one already secured, as shown in the picture (**N**). Neatly wrap the beading wire around all three wires between the two twists so that they are all bound securely in place (**O**). Continue this process, adding the T-shapes every 1cm (³/₈in). To add the small pearls, simply place them in position on the base of the crown and bind in their wires as you move along.

**2** To join the crown together, continue binding until you reach the end of the wire, then abut the two ends of the strong wire and continue binding the Ts until you reach your start point. Set aside.

**Note: the beaded crown and garland should be removed from the cake before it is carved.**

## colouring the staves

**1** Soften the dark brown modelling paste by kneading in some white vegetable fat then partially dunking the paste into boiled water before kneading again. Place the softened paste with the no. 0 tube into the sugar shaper. Take a fine paintbrush and paint sugar glue into the top embossed line on the treble stave.

**2** Starting with the tip of the tube on the embossed line, gently squeeze out the paste, moving the tip of the tube as you squeeze so that the paste falls into the embossed line. Repeat (**P**).

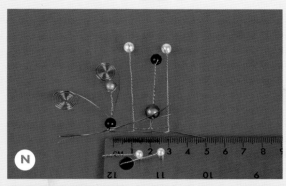

**N**

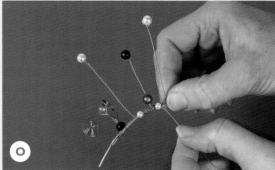

**O**

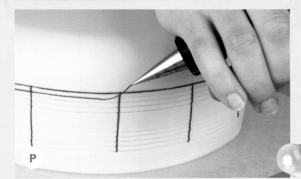

**P**

*You may find it easier to place your cake on a tilting turntable when adding the coloured lines to the staves.*

55

*If your bubbles are slightly pointed, quickly knock the point back into the bubble with a damp brush before the icing sets.*

## adding notes and clefs

1 Carefully remove a section of the musical notes from the plastic film. Dip a paintbrush in sugar glue and pick up the notes with the glued brush. Place in position on the appropriate stave and repeat to complete your musical composition (**Q**).

2 Randomly attach the musical notation onto the second tier with a glued paintbrush as shown in the main picture.

## assembling the cakes

Dowel and stack the cakes (see page 22).

## piping champagne bubbles

1 Divide the remaining royal icing into two and carefully colour each half to match approximately the sugarpaste colours of the second and top tier. Check the consistency, you need to be able to pipe bubbles not pointed cones.

2 Place a no 4 tube and some of the darker icing into a piping bag and pipe a few balls around the base of the second tier. Then pipe more using a no. 3, bringing the bubbles up the sides of the cake slightly. Change to a no. 2 tube and create lots of bubbles around the base and up the sides of both the second and top tiers. Add a few smaller bubbles to both tiers, with your choice of tube.

3 Pipe bubbles in the lighter shade of royal icing using tubes nos 0 and 2; add a few to the second tier to complement the darker bubbles and add the ones on the top tier to resemble bubbles rising up a champagne glass (**R**).

*Wash your brush immediately after painting with glaze.*

## attaching the crown

If necessary, adjust the shape of the base of the crown to create a circle. Then, using the royal icing already coloured to match the top tier, pipe icing along the underside of the crown. Place the crown centrally on top of the top tier. Take a damp paintbrush and neaten any visible royal icing, if necessary. Allow the icing to dry.

## finishing touches

1 Using a non-toxic glue stick attach the coffee ribbon around the side of the board to complete the cake.

2 Mix some edible antique gold dust with confectioners' glaze and use to paint over the musical notes and notation (**S**).

3 Once the royal icing that holds the crown in place has set, position and bend the beads and wires as desired.

## love the look

• coiled wire makes a covenient alternative to beads – try creating coils in different sizes for a funky look.
• piping bubbles in either toning or contrasting colours is a quick and easy way to add colour and texture to a plain cake.

## simple shortcuts

• Make the top two tiers; they will also be quicker and easier to decorate.
• Use the lower tier for a smaller but still intricately decorated cake with the topper added, or pipe a circle onto the top of the cake and fill it with piped champagne bubbles.
• Make the top cake, complete with champagne bubbles and its garland – ideal if you want to make the main decoration well in advance, as the piping is very simple.
• Any tier of the cake could be made separately. Add a simple beaded fountain or leave the top undecorated.

## small wonders

**These musical delights use the same sepia colours as the main cake and can be topped in a variety of ways for striking effects.**

Cut a cake into 4cm (1½in) deep slices. Using a 4.5cm (1¾in) circle cutter, cut the slices into rounds. It might be a good idea to bake slightly larger round cakes in the mini round tins that are now commercially available. Cover the cakes with the sepia colours used in the main cake. Then using pastillage and some musical cutters (FMM) cut out musical notes and a treble clef. Gild once dry, then attach to the tops of some of the cakes using royal icing. Pipe champagne bubbles onto the cakes, using the technique described for the main cake. Create mini garlands and crowns and place on the cakes as desired.

# snowflake

One of the many amazing natural wonders is the tiny snowflake – an individual crystalline work of art. This beautiful, glistening snowy-white cake, made from three carved and stacked round cakes, is covered in a flurry of snowflakes, each one with its own unique pattern. Made from pastillage and Artista soft, some of the snowflakes float on delicate crystal-decorated wires, and all are simply created using a variety of cutters. It has to be the most original cake to make for a winter wedding and is accompanied by dainty, snowy mini-cakes, below and on page 63.

## Or make this cake for …
• an extra-special Christmas cake (you could make a smaller version) • a special winter birthday celebration. • a skiing enthusiast.

# you will need...

## materials

- superwhite dust (SF) (optional)
- sugarpaste (rolled fondant): 2kg (4½lb) white
- 1 quantity of royal icing
- icing (confectioners') sugar (optional)
- white vegetable fat (shortening)
- cakes: 20cm (8in), 15cm (6in) and 10cm (4in) round (see pages 8–12)
- ½ quantity pastillage
- Artista soft (optional)
- buttercream, or apricot glaze and marzipan (see pages 16–17)
- clear spirit, such as gin or vodka
- dust colours: magic sparkles (SK) and/or white hologram (EA)

## equipment

- cake drums (boards): 25.5cm (10in) and 15cm (6in) round
- strong glue (optional)
- 5mm (³⁄₁₆in) spacers
- smoother
- palette knife
- narrow spacers made from 1.5mm (¹⁄₁₆in) thick card
- snowflake cutters, such as: starburst snowflake (LC), intricate snowflake (LC), simple snowflake (LC)
- craft knife
- selection of small cutters to remove patterns from the snowflakes, such as: small teardrop (LC), small triangle (LC), micro leaf cutter, small blossom
- foam pad
- quilting tool
- piping tubes (tips) nos: 16, 4, 3, 2, 1
- paintbrushes
- cocktail stick (toothpick)
- hardboard cake boards: 15cm (6in) and 10cm (4in) round
- 5cm (2in) round cake card (cut a larger one down to size)
- waxed paper
- dowels
- reusable piping bag and coupler
- glass-headed dressmakers' pins

## for the wired snowflakes

- 0.6mm width (23g SWG/22g AWG) silver-plated jewellery/hobby wire
- wire cutters
- strong acrylic glue
- 20 × 5mm (³⁄₁₆in) Swarovski cut-glass crystals
- posy pick
- oasis fix

# preparation

## colouring the paste

White sugarpaste tends to have a slightly off-white appearance due to the gums used in its manufacture, so if you wish your cake to look as pure white as snow then knead in some superwhite dust (edible whitening powder) to your sugarpaste.

## covering the board

1 Make 25.5cm (10in) and 15cm (6in) greaseproof paper circles by drawing around the cake drums. Fold the circles in half twice to find their centres.

2 Turn the 25.5cm (10in) cake drum over and mark its centre. Place the 15cm (6in) template centrally on the board by aligning the centres, and draw around the circle. Take the 15cm (6in) cake drum and stick it to the base of the board with strong glue or royal icing. This allows the board edges to be covered more easily with sugarpaste, making the cake easier to transport.

3 Roll out 750g (1lb 10oz) of white sugarpaste between 5mm (³⁄₁₆in) spacers using icing sugar or white vegetable fat to prevent sticking. Lift up the paste and place it over the board. Smooth the paste to give a level surface, then smooth the curved edge using the palm of your hand. Trim the sugarpaste flush with the underside of the board, taking care to keep the cut horizontal. Leave to dry.

## preparing the cakes for freezing

Level all the cakes and freeze (this step is optional but you will find carving frozen cakes a lot easier).

## making pastillage snowflakes

1 There are many different types of snowflakes with each one being unique, so below are some ideas for creating your own crystalline shapes.

2 Firstly, whiten the pastillage by kneading in some superwhite dust. Then use to create your crystals.

## snowflake 1

1 Roll out some of the paste between the narrow spacers. Pick up the paste and place it over the starburst snowflake cutter, then roll over the paste with a rolling pin (**A**). Run your finger over the edges of the cutter, then turn the cutter over and carefully press out the paste onto a well-greased work board. This gives you your outline shape.

2 Some snowflakes have what look like feathered edges; to create this on your snowflakes take a sharp craft knife and make repeated small cuts into the edges (**B**).

3 To remove some of the paste inside the shape, take a small teardrop cutter and cut out six shapes radiating out from the centre (**C**).

4 Leave the snowflakes on your work board until the paste has hardened, to prevent them distorting. Place on a foam pad and dry thoroughly. (An airing cupboard is an ideal place to dry pastillage, as the gentle heat removes moisture).

## snowflake 2

1 Cut out a snowflake shape, as before, using the intricate snowflake cutter (**D**).

2 Take a quilting tool and run it across the resulting snowflake from point to opposite point to add texture to its surface (**E**).

3 Cut a circle from the centre of each of the six inner sections, as defined by the quilting tool, using the end of a no. 16 piping tube (**F**).

## other snowflakes

To create other variations, use any small cutters that you may have to remove sections of paste. Remember that you can combine or overlap cutters to create different shapes and that you can remove paste away from the outline of the shape using a part of a cutter, see the finished snowflake pictures for inspiration (**G**).

## making the wired snowflakes

1 It is best to make these from Artista soft, a non-toxic modelling medium made from potato and rice flour that is extremely lightweight and has the huge advantage of not breaking when knocked or dropped.

2 Make the snowflakes in exactly the same way as for the pastillage ones but leave them on your well-greased work board to dry thoroughly before removing them, to prevent them curling. Once dry, remove the snowflakes from the board with a palette knife and neaten any fibrous edges by running a wet paintbrush over the fibres.

## making beaded wires

1 Cut various lengths of silver-plated jewellery wire. Then, using strong acrylic glue, attach a snowflake to one end of each length of wire.

2 Once the glue has set, use a cocktail stick to place a dot of glue onto the wire further down from the snowflake and then slide a crystal onto the glue to attach it to the wire. Repeat, adding two to four crystals to each wire (**H**). Leave to dry.

# stage one

## carving the cakes

1 Level the cakes if not already done so in the preparation stage. Turn the base cake over, so that it rests on its levelled top. Then take the 15cm (6in) round hardboard cake board and place it in the centre of the base. With a knife make a shallow cut around the board to mark its position, so that if the board slips it is easier to replace.

2 Next, carve from the edge of the board down to the outside edge of the cake (the surface that is resting on your work surface). Do this in small cuts to ensure that you don't carve away too much cake (**I**).

3 Turn the cake back over, and straighten the cut of the sides if necessary. Also check that the cake is symmetrical and adjust as required. Take a small knife and carefully curve the top edge (**J**). Repeat for the smaller cakes, using the 10cm (4in) cake board for the 15cm (6in) cake and 5cm (2in) cake card for the 10cm (4in) cake.

## covering the cakes

1 Stick the 20cm (8in) cake onto the 15cm (6in) cake board, using apricot glaze or buttercream as appropriate, and then place on waxed paper.

2 If using a fruit cake cover with apricot glaze and marzipan, then follow directions for the sugarpaste covering below.

3 To help the sugarpaste stick to the cake, cover with a thin layer of buttercream (for a sponge cake) or paint over the marzipan with clear spirit (for a fruit cake). Roll out 1kg (2¼lb) of whitened sugarpaste and use to cover the cake. Carefully ease in the fullness of paste around the sides of the cake. Start near the top of the sides and, using a cupped hand, stroke the paste in an upward direction, gradually lowering your hand down the sides until all the paste is eased in. Be careful, as you don't want any pleats. If the paste seems to be forming a pleat, lift up the sugarpaste around the pleat to redistribute the paste and try again.

4 Smooth the sugarpaste, by firstly using a smoother to iron out any irregulars in the surface of the icing and then using the base of your hand to smooth and polish the top edge. Take the smoother and, while pressing down, run the flat edge around the base of the cake to create a cutting line. Cut away the excess paste with a palette knife. Repeat for the remaining tiers, placing the cakes individually on waxed paper with the respective cake boards underneath each cake before covering. Set the cakes aside to dry.

# stage two

## assembling the cakes

Dowel and stack the cakes centrally on the covered board (see page 22). Insert a posy pick into the centre of the top tier (**K**), then add a sausage of oasis fix into the posy pick to help secure the wired snowflakes.

## piping royal icing snow

1 Whiten the royal icing by mixing in a little superwhite. Check the consistency of your icing and adjust as necessary – you need to be able to pipe dots, not pointed cones.

2 Fit the no. 16 tube into the coupler on the reusable piping bag and half-fill the bag with the whitened icing. Pipe a few dots around the base of each tier, then change the tube size to a no. 4 and pipe more dots to help disguise the joins between the tiers. Keep changing the tube to smaller sizes and piping dots until the piped dots encircle all of the cakes (**L**).

## adding the pastillage snowflakes

Carefully attach the dried pastillage snowflakes to the cake using royal icing. Try to position them so that they look as if they are drifting down the cake. Support the snowflakes on the sides of the cake with pins to prevent them slipping down the sides of the cake before the royal icing has set (**M**). Remove the pins once secure.

L

## adding more snow

1 Pipe royal icing dots in varying sizes randomly around the snowflakes to emphasise the drifting snow (**N**). Allow the icing to set.

2 Dust the cake and snowflakes with either or both of the suggested dusts to add a real sparkle to the appearance of the cake (**O**).

## arranging the floating snowflakes

Take one of the wired snowflakes and bend the wire to make smooth curves in different directions, referring to the finished cake for guidance. Then insert the end into the posy pick and position as desired. Continue bending the wires and adding snowflakes until you are happy with the appearance of the cake (**P**).

## love the look

• Add the snowflakes and drifting snow to a shop-bought cake of any shape or size.

• If you prefer more colour, make the snowflakes in different shades, such as ice blue, sparkling gold or a striking red.

• The piped drifting snow could be used to decorate any cake.

• Cover a shop-bought cake with coloured sugarpaste and add a few snowflakes, so that they will really stand out.

## simple shortcuts

• Make a smaller cake by using just the top two tiers.

• Use stacked, round cakes without carving them.

• Cover the cake with pastillage snowflakes without the wired snowflake decoration.

• Make an extra-simple version with just the iced snow along the joins and randomly over the cake.

## small wonders

**Make these snowy-white wintery gems, each with an individual snowflake, for Christmas or as seasonal wedding gifts.**

Bake your cakes in 5cm (2in) multimini cake pans or cut a larger cake into 5cm (2in) deep slices and then, using a 5cm (2in) circle cutter, cut the slices into rounds. Cover the cakes with the white sugarpaste used for the main cake. Decorate each cake with a pastillage snowflake and a drift of royal icing dots. Add sparkle by dusting the cakes with either or both of the suggested edible dusts.

63

# connoisseur's delight

Create this smart presentation box of fine wines as a birthday, celebration or retirement gift for a connoisseur or wine enthusiast. A simple arrangement of stacked rectangular cakes forms the box, which has rounded bottles made in relief from modelling paste on the front. Painted realistically, the bottles appear to contain wine and are complete with gilded foils and aged labels to add an authentic touch. Although the details might seem complicated they can all be copied from magazine pictures or the Internet, or you can even make a simplified version. For an attractive finish wired beads are arranged stylishly to top the box.

The matching mini-cakes, see below and page 71, make inspiring gifts for wine lovers.

## Or make this cake for …
• an avid crossword or sudoku puzzler, by simply making modelling-paste squares and using cut-out letters and numbers • someone who likes bold designs, by using cut-out circles, geometric shapes or flowers in vivid colours • a garden-lover by adding painted and cut-out flowers, leaves and butterflies.

# you will need ...

## materials

- sugarpaste (rolled fondant): 1kg (2¼lb) burgundy, 1.1kg (2½lb) bottle green, 1.4kg (3lb 1oz) ivory, 700g (1½lb) gold
- icing (confectioners') sugar
- white vegetable fat (shortening)
- 2 quantities buttercream, or apricot glaze and marzipan (see pages 16–17)
- cakes: two 18cm × 23cm (7 × 9in) rectangular Madeira or chocolate (these are cut down), or two 15 × 20cm (6 × 8in) fruit cakes (see pages 8–12)
- clear spirit, such as gin or vodka
- sugar glue (see page 14)
- modelling paste: 115g (4oz) bottle green, 25g (1oz) ivory, 25g (1oz) cream, 25g (1oz), deep red, 175g (6oz) burgundy, 50g (2oz) golden brown, 175g (6oz) olive green
- paste colours: mint green, olive green, burgundy, golden brown (Spectral autumn leaf), cream, red, black
- edible dust colours: bronze, selection of golds
- confectioners' glaze

## equipment

- 30cm (12in) round cake drum (board)
- greaseproof paper
- 5mm (³⁄₁₆in) spacers
- smoother
- palette knife
- scriber
- glass-headed dressmakers' pins
- straightedge, such as a ruler
- dowels (if using sponge cake)
- 15 × 10cm (6 × 4in) hardboard cake board (if using sponge cake)
- waxed paper and scissors
- tracing paper
- set square
- narrow spacers – made from thick card
- craft knife
- cutting wheel
- Dresden tool
- paintbrushes
- piping tubes: nos 4 and 18
- small embosser, such as Embossing Sticks – set 2 (HP) (optional)
- burgundy ribbon, thin gold ribbon and non-toxic glue stick

## for the beaded topper

- posy pick
- 0.6mm (23g SWG/22g AWG) gold jewellery wire
- a selection of green, gold and burgundy beads; Lindy used:
  - 35 deep red oval glass pearls
  - 32 × 6mm (¼in) deep gold glass pearls
  - 9 × 8mm (⁵⁄₁₆in) bottle-green wooden beads
  - lime-green and bottle-green silver-lined rocailles
- wire cutter
- gold crimps
- pliers
- oasis fix

# preparation

### covering the board

**1** Put the cake drum onto a sheet of greaseproof paper and draw around its edge. Fold the circle in half and half again to find its centre.

**2** Knead the burgundy sugarpaste then roll out between 5mm (³⁄₁₆in) spacers using icing sugar or white vegetable fat to prevent sticking. Lift up the paste, place over the board and smooth it level. Trim the edges flush with the sides using a palette knife.

**3** Mark the centre of the covered board with a scriber or pin using the greaseproof circle as a template. Take the straightedge and indent a line to divide the circle in half. Indent a line at 90 degrees to the first. Fill between two opposing quarters with lines that radiate out from the central point (**A**); space the lines at the edge of the circle about 1cm (³⁄₈in) apart. Neaten the edge of the board then leave to dry.

# stage one

## carving the cake

**1** **Madeira or chocolate cakes**
Take a large knife and carefully remove the crusts from the sides of both cakes (**B**). Cut each cake in half along the long edge to give a total of four cakes measuring about 15 x 10cm (6 x 4in). Level the top of each section of cake by placing the cakes on one long edge and making a vertical cut (**C**).

**2** **Sponge cakes** If using the sponge recipes in this book, cover the tops of two cakes with buttercream or jam and stack three cakes to make a tower. Insert four dowels down through the cake (see page 22), then cover the top of the stack with buttercream. Place the remaining cake onto the 15 x 10cm

*A set square will help ensure the sides of your cake are vertical.*

*It is worthwhile spending time getting the shape correct, as this greatly affects the overall appearance of the cake.*

(6 x 4in) hardboard cake board and position it on top of the stack. (For softer sponge, you may need to dowel each layer individually.)

**3** Use a knife to adjust the sides of the tower so that they are all vertical and the corners square (**D**).

**4** **Fruit cakes:** Turn the cakes upside down, so that the flat surface is uppermost. Trim the sides of the cakes, if necessary, so that they are vertical. Cut each cake in half along the long edge to give a total of four cakes measuring about 15 x 10cm (6 x 4in). Spread a layer of apricot glaze over the top of three cakes and stack all the cakes to make a tower. Use marzipan to fill any gaps between the layers. Trim the sides of the tower as for the sponge cake.

## covering the cake

**1** If using fruit cake, cover with apricot glaze and marzipan, keeping the corners sharp, following instructions for sugarpaste below.

**2** Place the fruit or sponge stacked cake on waxed paper so that it rests on one of the largest sides – the back or front of the cake.

**3** Knead the bottle-green sugarpaste until warm. Roll just over half into a roughly rectangular shape between 5mm (³/₁₆in) spacers. Cut one long edge straight.

**4** To help the sugarpaste stick to sponge cake, cover one narrow side of the cake with a thin layer of buttercream. For fruit cake, paint one narrow marzipan side with clear spirit.

**5** Lift the green sugarpaste over a rolling pin, and position over the side of the cake, placing the straight edge against the lower edge of the cake. Use a smoother with a circular motion to smooth the paste evenly.

**6** Roughly cut away the excess paste with a pair of scissors to remove the excess weight (**E**).

**7** Place the smoother onto the surface of the green sugarpaste so that it slightly overhangs the edge of the cake then, using a palette knife, remove the excess paste by cutting away from the cake onto the smoother (**F**). Repeat for the second green side.

**8** Cover the uppermost side with ivory sugarpaste, cutting to shape as before, although this time you will have to cut upwards against the smoother. Try to keep the join between the two coloured pastes neat.

**9** Move the cake back into its upright position and cover the remaining side and top with ivory sugarpaste. Allow to dry.

# stage two

### tracing the design

Using tracing paper, trace the design on page 133. Retrace the lines onto the back of the paper then temporarily fix the tracing to the front of the cake with pins. Transfer only the traced bottle outlines onto the cake by going over the outlines again with a sharp pencil. Repeat for the back of the cake, if you like.

*You can personalize your cake by using the recipient's favourite wines or drink. Find pictures of the bottles in magazines or on the Web, and create your own montage.*

### adding the lid

1 Scribe a horizontal line onto each green side of the cake to mark the lid of the box, using a set square and the traced design on the front and back as a guide (**G**).

2 Knead the gold sugarpaste, then roll out some into a rectangular shape between 5mm (³/₁₆in) spacers. Cut one long edge straight. Paint over the narrow green sides of the lid with sugar glue, then place the cut edge along one of the scribed lines. Cut away the majority of the excess paste with scissors then cut to shape by using a smoother and palette knife (**H**). Cover the other narrow end, followed by the two sides ensuring that the corners of the lid remain sharp.

3 To emboss the lid, mark near the outside edges of each face at 5mm (³/₁₆in) vertical intervals using a ruler and scriber. Line up the marks horizontally with a straightedge, and emboss the sugarpaste repeatedly to create the textured pattern of the lid (**I**). Repeat for the remaining sides.

4 Cover the top of the cake, neatening the cut edges so that they become part of the pattern of the lid.

5 To insert the posy pick, measure the top of the lid and make a greaseproof paper template the same size. Fold it into quarters to find the centre. Place the template onto the cake and mark the centre with a scriber. Insert the posy pick vertically into the centre of the cake (**J**) so that its top lies flush with the top of the lid.

### adding the bottles

1 Start with the top line of bottles and complete the ones in the background before the ones in the foreground. Then make the lower bottles, completing the foreground bottles last.

2 Select a bottle and cut its shape out from the tracing made earlier. Roll out some modelling paste to the required depth – the background bottles need to be about 1mm (¹/₃₂in) thick whereas the large foreground bottle on the right-hand side should be about 5mm (³/₁₆in); all the others should be thicknesses in between. Place the bottle tracing on top of the rolled-out paste and cut around the shape with a cutting wheel (**K**). Cut away the neck of the bottle and round the sides by rubbing your fingers along the cut edges (**L**). Attach in place on the cake with sugar glue.

3 Add a bottle neck where necessary, by adding a strip of paste the same thickness as the bottle to the top of the neck; smooth and blend into the surface of the bottle. Complete all the bottles before creating their tops.

4 For the foils, take your chosen colour of modelling paste and roll out to a thickness slightly greater than for the bottle you are placing it on. Cut out the required shape using the tracing template and a craft knife, then round the side and top edges with a finger.

**G**

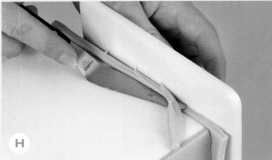

**H**

**I**

**J**

**K**

**L**

**5** Stick the foil in place and indent the top of the bottle's neck with a cutting wheel (**M**). Using a Dresden tool enlarge this indentation and adjust the outline shape of the bottle top (**N**).

**6** To create the textured top of the champagne foil, press into the top of the foil paste with a Dresden tool (**O**), then press in the sides to create the characteristic shape.

## painting the bottles

(If you are running out of time, painting the bottles is not essential.)

**1** In a paint palette separately dilute some mint green, olive green and burgundy paste colours with clear spirit or boiled water. Then, with a paintbrush, carefully apply vertical strokes of colour. Aim for a streaked effect to represent light reflecting off the bottles (**P**).

**2** Paint the red foils in a similar fashion with the burgundy paste colour. Allow the painted bottles to dry.

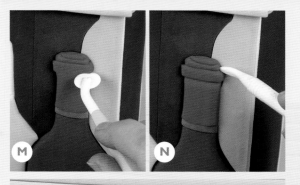

# stage three

## making the labels

**1** Using the bottle tracings, scribe the top line of each label onto the cake as a guide to placement.

**2** Working on one label at a time, cut out the label from the bottle tracing and place onto thinly rolled ivory or cream modelling paste. Cut around the template with a craft knife

and stick the resulting shape in place on the appropriate bottle.

**3** To add texture to some of the labels, use the ends of piping tubes or small stick embossers (**Q**) to add a pattern. The circle on the large right-hand bottle is made from a circle of golden-brown modelling paste embossed with a button.

**4** Separately dilute some brown and cream paste colour and apply a vertical wash over the labels. Allow to dry.

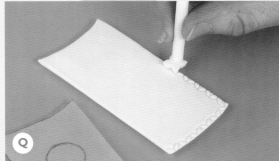

# stage four

## painting the labels

Using the bottle tracings, transfer each label's detail to the cake using a sharp pencil. Separately dilute a selection of colours then, using a fine paintbrush, add the painted detail to the labels (**R**).

*There is a lot of scope for personalizing the cake by adding names, dates, and so on.*

## gilding the lid

1 Mix a little bronze edible lustre dust with some confectioners' glaze and use to paint over one of the bottle tops. Individually mix up the various golds and colour the remaining bottle tops. Take a fine paintbrush and add gold detail to the labels and foils as required.

2 Mix up a larger quantity of dark/antique gold and, using a flat-headed brush, paint the lid of the box using long horizontal strokes (**S**).

## adding ribbon and topper

Roll out some burgundy modelling paste into a strip between the narrow spacers. Using a cutting wheel and a straightedge, cut out a 2.5cm (1in) wide strip. Place the strip centrally over the lid. Glue the sides in place just under the lid and cut to size. Emboss each end of the ribbon using a no. 4 tube. Remove a circle of paste directly above the posy pick using a no. 18 tube. Add the beaded topper (see below).

*Clean your brush immediately after painting with glaze.*

## finishing touches

1 Roll out some bottle-green modelling paste into a strip between the narrow spacers. Using a cutting wheel and a straightedge cut out four 8mm (⁵⁄₁₆in) wide strips. Paint glue along the vertical edges of the green sides and position the strips on top of the glue to hide the ivory edges. Cut to fit.

2 Using a non-toxic glue stick attach the burgundy and gold ribbons around the sides of the board to complete the cake.

## the beaded topper

1 Cut six 60cm (23⁵⁄₈in) lengths of gold jewellery wire. Select three different arrangements of beads of your own choice, using the suggested beads as a guide.

2 For a single bead arrangement, as shown in the picture, thread 1 crimp onto a prepared wire, then alternately thread one bead followed

by 2 crimps. You will need a total of about 9 beads. Position the first crimp 8cm (3⅛in) from one end of the wire and squeeze it onto the wire using pliers. Move the nearest bead and next crimp up to the first crimp. Squeeze the second crimp in place, so that the bead cannot move along the wire. Leave a gap of about 1.5cm (⁹⁄₁₆in) and repeat (**T**) until you have secured all the beads.

3 Bend the ends of the wire over so that the beaded section forms a circle, and twist the ends together to form a stem. Repeat for your remaining bead selections. Then wire up a single large green bead by threading it onto a short length of wire and twisting the ends of the wire together.

4 Place a small sausage of oasis fix into the posy pick. Place the stems of the beaded circles into the posy pick so that the circles sit opposite each other in a spiral petal pattern (see below). Place the wired green bead in the centre.

## love the look

- Gilding provides a luxurious highlight for even the plainest of cakes – add it just around the sides or edges.
- A simple strip of sugarpaste makes a pretty ribbon around any shape of cake.

## simple shortcuts

- Leave the bottles unpainted for a quick but effective version.
- Make a modelling-paste bow rather than the beaded topper.
- Simplify the labels on the bottles.
- Omit the ridges on the box top.
- Use a plain cake board without the radiating lines.
- Omit the sugarpaste ribbon and wired topper and attach a fabric ribbon to the box with a bow on top.

# small wonders

**For those who enjoy a smaller tipple, these mini-cakes follow the same techniques of cutting out and labelling the bottles as for the main cake.**

Cut a cake into 9 x 3.5 x 3cm (3½in x 1³/₈in x 1¹/₈in) portions and cover each portion as for the main cake. Using a small bottle cutter (PC), cut out a selection of bottles from suitable coloured modelling paste. Separately cut out labels and foils in appropriate colours, then use these to replace the label and foil section on the cut out bottle. Stick the bottles to the front of the mini-cakes and paint the labels and foils as for the main cake, following the instructions for the main cake.

# funky
# flowers

Shocking pink, luminous orange and bright yellow shout out from this vibrant cake made from stacked square cakes cut at angles to give an entirely individual effect. It's an original cake to give someone who likes something different. Bold statements and wild colours create simple but eye-catching decorations, which are all made using cutters. What makes them so effective is the combination of large, colourful shapes and smaller areas of interlocking coloured pastes. A perfect replica of the main cake can be created as a funky mini-cake (see below and page 77).

## Or make this cake for …
• a fun-loving and extrovert couple's wedding
• an individual and outgoing girl on her eighteenth birthday.

73

# you will need ...

## materials

- sugarpaste (rolled fondant): 1.5kg (3lb 3oz) orange, 1.2kg (2lb 10oz) red, 400g (14oz) pink

- icing (confectioners') sugar (optional)

- white vegetable fat (shortening)

- cakes: 25.5cm (10in), 18cm (7in) and 10cm (4in) square (see pages 8–12)

- buttercream, or apricot glaze and marzipan (see pages 16–17)

- a little boiled jam (if using fruit cake)

- clear spirit, such as gin or vodka (if using fruit cakes)

- ¼ quantity of royal icing

- modelling paste: 50g (2oz) red, 50g (2oz) orange, 115g (4oz) pink, 25g (1oz) yellow, 25g (1oz) purple

- sugar glue (see page 14)

## equipment

- 5mm (³/₁₆in) spacers

- 33cm (13in) round cake drum (board)

- smoother

- palette knife

- hardboard square cake boards: 20cm (8in), 13cm (5in)

- waxed paper

- 7.5cm (3in) cake card (cut a larger one down to size)

- dowels

- sugar shaper and medium round disc

- fine paintbrush

- craft knife

- Dresden tool

- narrow spacers made from 1.5mm (¹/₁₆in) thick card

- circle cutters: 2.5cm (1in), 4.5cm (1¾in) (FMM geometric set)

- daisy centre stamps (JEM)

- flower cutters: 10cm (4in) large five-petal blossom cutter (OP-F6C), six-petal flower from flat floral collection set 2 (LC), large flat floral set (LC)

- clear plastic, such as a plastic bag

- piping tubes (tips) nos 18, 16, 4 (PME)

- orange ribbon and non-toxic glue stick

*Make 5mm (³/₁₆in) spacers from strip wood.*

# preparation

### covering the board
Roll out 1kg (2¼lb) of orange sugarpaste between 5mm (³/₁₆in) spacers using icing sugar or white vegetable fat to prevent sticking. Lift up the paste and place over the cake drum. Use a smoother to smooth the paste level. Trim the edges flush with the sides of the board using a palette knife. Place to one side to dry.

### preparing the cakes
(If time is short this can all be done at stage one.) Referring to page 19, you can use either a 7.5cm (3in) or 10cm (4in) deep cake. Level the cake you are using then follow the instructions for your size below:

### for 7.5cm (3in) deep cakes
**1** Take one of the cakes, (the pictures show the 18cm (7in) cake) and place it on one of its sides.

Take a long-bladed, sharp knife and a ruler, and vertically make a cut diagonally through the cake from the top corner on one side to 2.5cm (1in) below the top corner on the other (**A**). Carefully remove the tapered slice and place it onto a cake board with the cut side uppermost, then turn the main section of cake back onto its base.

2 Spread buttercream (if using a sponge cake) or boiled jam (if using a fruit cake) over the sloping top of the main cake.

3 Carefully slide the top section of cake from its board onto the prepared surface of the main cake so that the two highest and two lowest sides match, giving the cake greater height and an increase in the angle of the slope. Freeze the cakes.

## for 10cm (4in) deep cakes

Follow the instructions above but make the diagonal cut 5cm (2in) deep and remove the tapered slice. Freeze the cakes.

# stage one

## carving the cakes

1 Make three square paper templates, measuring 20cm (8in), 14cm (5½in) and 6.5cm (2½in). Turn one of the frozen cakes over (the pictures show the 18cm (7in) cake), so that it rests on its top sloping side. Take the square paper template of the correct size – for example, for the 18cm (7in) cake, take the 14cm (5½in) square – and place it in the centre of the cake.

2 With a knife make a shallow cut around the square to mark its position. Carve from the edge of the template down to the outside edge of the cake, which is resting on your work surface (**B**).

3 Take a small knife and curve the edges and corners (**C**). Repeat for the remaining cakes

## covering the cakes

1 Stick the 25.5cm (10in) cake onto the 20cm (8in) board, using apricot glaze or buttercream, then place on waxed paper. Cover a fruit cake with apricot glaze and marzipan; follow directions for sugarpaste.

2 To help the sugarpaste stick to the cake, cover with a thin layer of buttercream or clear spirit as appropriate. Roll out the red sugarpaste and use to cover the cake, being careful not to stretch the paste over the corners. If the paste seems to be forming a pleat, lift up the sugarpaste around the pleat to redistribute the paste, and try again.

3 Use a smoother to smooth the sugarpaste, then use the base of your hand to smooth and polish the top and corner edges. Run the flat edge of the smoother around the base of the cake to create a cutting line. Cut away the excess paste with a palette knife.

4 Stick the 18cm (7in) cake onto the 13cm (5in) cake board and place on waxed paper. Cover the cake with a thin layer of buttercream or clear spirit as appropriate. Cover the cake using the orange sugarpaste.

5 Stick the 10cm (4in) cake onto the cake card and place on waxed paper. Cover with the pink sugarpaste. Leave to dry.

# stage two

## stacking the cakes

1 Remove the base tier from its waxed paper and place it centrally on the prepared cake drum. Dowel the base and second tiers (see page 22).

2 Using a small amount of royal icing, attach the middle tier centrally on top of the base tier so that its lowest side is above one of the tallest corners of the base tier. Now attach the top tier to the middle tier, lining it up so that its lowest side is above one of the middle tier's tallest corners – you are aiming for a corkscrew effect (see the main picture for guidance).

## adding trim

1 Soften some red modelling paste by kneading in some white vegetable fat and then partially dunking the paste into a small container of boiled water. Knead the paste again (it should have the consistency of chewing gum). Put the paste into the sugar shaper with the medium round disc.

2 With a fine paintbrush paint a line of sugar glue around the base of the larger cake. Squeeze out a long length of paste and carefully

place it around the base of the cake. Cut both ends of paste at 45 degrees using a craft knife so that the two ends will fit snugly. Glue the ends together and blend the join with the wide end of a Dresden tool. Repeat, using orange for the middle tier and pink for the upper tier.

## decorating the base tier

1 Take some yellow modelling paste and knead the paste to warm it (add a little white fat and/or boiled water, if necessary, to soften). The paste should be firm but with some elasticity. Roll out the paste between narrow spacers and cut out seven 4.5cm (1¾in) circles for the flower centres.

2 Take the three smallest daisy centre stamps and randomly emboss the yellow paste circles by pressing down hard on the stamps but taking care not to cut all the way through the paste (**D**).

3 Attach one to each side of the cake and three to the top using sugar glue, leaving enough space between each to allow the petals to fit without touching (use the large five-petal blossom cutter as a guide to help you). Where the circles on the sides abut the base, cut across part of the circle with a craft knife to achieve a snug fit.

4 Roll out the pink modelling paste between narrow spacers and cut out seven large flowers using the large blossom cutter.

*If the cut is not clean around the petals use a craft knife to cut cleanly around the outside edge of the cut flower.*

5 Leave the flowers on your work surface and remove the excess paste. Take the 4.5cm (1¾in) circle cutter and cut out a circle from the centre of each flower (**E**).

6 Attach the petals to the cake, positioning them evenly around each of the yellow circles and leaving a 5mm (³⁄₁₆in) gap between the centre and the petals.

7 Roll out the orange modelling paste between narrow spacers and cut out seven six-petal flowers from the flat floral collection. Next, take a craft knife and cut the flowers into individual petals (**F**). Attach to the cake, positioning one between each large, pink petal.

## decorating the middle tier

1 Roll out the different colours of modelling paste between narrow spacers and cover with plastic to prevent them drying out. Using the 4.5cm (1¾in) circle cutter, cut a circle from one of the pastes. Leave the circle where it was cut and carefully remove the excess paste, to prevent the circle distorting.

2 Take the 2.5cm (1in) circle cutter and remove a circle from the centre of the larger one.

*A scriber is an excellent tool to help remove the cut circles.*

3 Replace this circle with one of a different colour, and blend the join between the two circles by rubbing a finger over the pastes so that there is no gap between them (**G**).

4 Continue removing and replacing circles of different colours using the piping tubes as circle cutters. Attach the concentric circles to the middle tier using sugar glue.

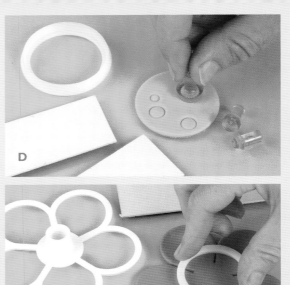
D

E

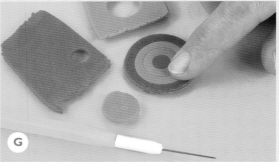
F

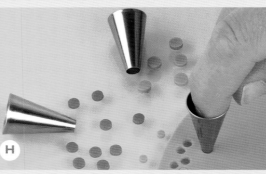
G

H

I

# stage three

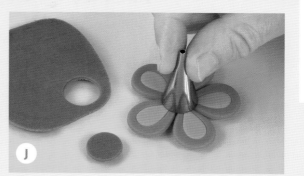

5 Make a selection of concentric circles in different sizes and colours, referring to the finished cake pictures. Attach to the cake. Where the circles on the sides abut the base cake, cut across a section of the circle with a craft knife for a close fit.

6 Using the piping tubes, cut small circles of paste in different colours and sizes (**H**) and attach them around the outside of some of the circles on the cake.

## decorating the top tier

1 Roll out the red modelling paste between narrow spacers and cut out five flowers using the large flat floral set.

2 Using the teardrop cutter from the large flat floral set remove the centre of each petal (**I**). Replace the teardrops with orange ones cut from thinly rolled paste. Blend the join between the two pastes by rubbing a finger over it.

3 Now remove the centre from the flower with the wide end of a

piping tube (**J**) and replace it with a purple one. Blend the join. Attach one of the completed flowers to the top of the cake on the largest side. Then cut across part of each remaining flower with a craft knife to allow them to fit the remaining sides (refer to the pictures as a guide).

## finishing touches
Using a non-toxic glue stick attach the ribbon around the sides of the board to complete the cake.

## love the look
• The bold flowers or circles would brighten up any cake and would work just as well made using modelling paste in subtle pastel shades.
• Use the contrasting bright colours of pink and orange on a simple cake by covering it with sugarpaste in one colour and then decorating it with simple cut-out shapes in the other.

## simple shortcuts
• Make a wonky single-layer cake from the base layer.
• Use square shop-bought cakes without cutting the tops at angles, and arrange them so that each layer is slightly off-centre and rotated, to add a sense of fun.
• For a quick decoration that's still eye-catching, cover the cake with the large pink flowers with yellow centres, as these are the simplest to make.

## small wonders

**If you know someone who's a little on the wild side make them the perfect gift by creating this miniature reproduction of the main cake.**
Carve your mini-cakes from 9cm (3½in), 6cm (2⅜in) and 3cm (1⅛in) squares of cake. Make the heights of the cakes 6.5cm (2½in), 5cm (2in) and 3.5cm (1⅜in) respectively, then build and decorate as the main cake. You can vary the colour combination, as in the picture; the pink makes an especially attention-grabbing colour for the main part of the cake. Top it with a circle of cut-out shapes and a colour-coordinated candle to finish off.

# greek inspirations

Recreate the symmetry of ancient Greek architecture and design, found in ceramics and jewellery, with this unique, square stacked cake – perfect for lovers of Greece. The warm and traditional colours of light gold, terracotta and navy blue are used to create bold triangles and the classical palmette motif – a fan-shaped ornamental pattern that resembles a palm leaf and is a symbol of peace. Gold trims and scrolls add a touch of grandeur, but because most of the decoration is made using cut-out shapes the stunning effect is simple to achieve. Accompany the cake with some miniature cake gift 'boxes' (see below and page 83).

## Or make this cake for ...

• a bon voyage gift for someone who is moving to the Mediterranean • a celebration cake for someone who has passed exams • someone who has Greek roots or who loves Greece.

# you will need ...

## materials

- sugarpaste (rolled fondant): 1kg (2¼lb) navy blue, 1.5kg (3lb 5oz) light gold

*Use Spectral colours autumn leaf to make a gold-coloured paste.*

- icing (confectioners') sugar (optional)
- white vegetable fat (shortening)
- cakes: 23cm (9in) square cake × 3.5cm (1⅜in) deep, 15cm (6in) square cake × 10cm (4in) deep (see pages 8–12)

*If you don't have a cake tin (pan) deep enough, bake two shallower cakes and stack them together.*

- buttercream, or apricot glaze and marzipan (see pages 16–17)
- clear spirit, such as gin or vodka
- gum tragacanth
- ¼ quantity of royal icing
- sugar glue (see page 14)
- modelling paste:100g (3½oz) terracotta, 100g (3½oz) antique gold to match dust
- edible dust colours: antique gold (SK)
- confectioners' glaze

## equipment

- 5mm (³⁄₁₆in) spacers
- 30cm (12in) square cake drum (board)
- smoother
- palette knife
- Greek motif embosser – set 2, side designs (HP)
- hardboard cake boards: 23cm (9in) and 15cm (6in) square
- waxed paper
- dowels
- sugar shaper with small and medium round discs
- paintbrush
- craft knife
- Dresden tool
- piping tubes (tips) nos 18, 17, 16, 3
- narrow spacers made from 1.5mm (¹⁄₁₆in) thick card
- cutters: equilateral triangles (LC), circle, large teardrop set (LC), small teardrop set (LC)
- set square
- scriber
- glass-headed dressmakers' pins
- navy-blue and thin gold ribbon and non-toxic glue stick

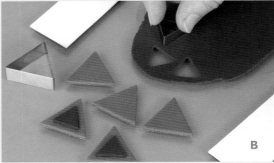

# preparation

### covering the board

1 Knead the navy-blue sugarpaste to warm. Then roll the paste out between 5mm (³⁄₁₆in) spacers using icing sugar or white vegetable fat to prevent sticking, and use to cover the cake drum. Trim the edges flush with the sides of the board using a palette knife, taking care to keep the cut vertical.

2 Position the smoother vertically against the edge of the board then place the embosser up against the smoother and press it into the soft paste. Line up the embosser so that the next embossed shape will be adjacent to the first, and press down (**A**). Repeat until you have embossed all around the edge of the board. Place to one side to dry.

# stage one

## covering the cakes

1 Stick the 15cm (6in) cake onto the hardboard cake board of the same size, using apricot glaze or buttercream as appropriate, then place on waxed paper.

2 If using a fruit cake, carefully cover with apricot glaze and marzipan then follow directions for sugarpaste below.

3 To help the sugarpaste stick to the cake, cover with a thin layer of buttercream (for a sponge cake) or paint over the marzipan with clear spirit (for a fruit cake).

4 Roll out 1kg (2¼lb) of light-gold sugarpaste and use to cover the cake. Carefully ease in the fullness of paste around the corners of the cake. Start near the top and, using a cupped hand, stroke the paste in an upward direction then gradually lower your hand until all the paste is eased in. Be careful, as you don't want any pleats. If the paste seems to be forming a pleat, then lift up the sugarpaste around the pleat to redistribute the paste and try again.

## finishing the surface

1 Smooth the sugarpaste by using a smoother to iron out any irregulars in the surface of the icing and then use the base of your hand to smooth and polish the top edge. Take the smoother and, while pressing down, run the flat edge around the base of the cake to create a cutting line. Cut away the excess paste with a palette knife.

2 Stick the 23cm (9in) cake onto the hardboard cake board of the same size, then place on a piece of waxed paper and cover with the remaining light-gold sugarpaste.

## making modelling paste

Take 100g (3½oz) of the gold and navy-blue sugarpaste trimmings and knead in 2.5ml (½ tsp) gum tragacanth to each colour to make modelling paste. Leave the paste to mature, ideally overnight.

*If you are pushed for time, use CMC instead of gum tragacanth, as it reacts much quicker.*

# stage two

## assembling the cakes

Dowel and stack the cakes (see page 22) using royal icing to secure.

## adding trim

1 Soften some gold modelling paste. Do this by firstly kneading in some white vegetable fat to stop the paste getting sticky and then partially dunk the paste into a small container of boiled water before kneading again (the paste should have the consistency of chewing gum). Place the softened paste with the medium round disc into the sugar shaper.

2 Take a fine paintbrush and, using some sugar glue, paint a line of glue around the base of the 15cm (6in) cake. Squeeze out a long length of paste from the shaper and carefully place it around the base of the cake. Cut one end at 45 degrees, using a craft knife, then cut the other end also at 45 degrees so that the two ends will sit snugly together. Glue the ends together using sugar glue and blend the join neatly with the wide end of a Dresden tool.

3 Take a no. 3 piping tube and press it repeatedly into the trim to create a textured finish.

## adding the border decoration to the base tier

1 Thinly roll out some terracotta and navy-blue modelling pastes between narrow spacers. Take the largest triangle from the equilateral triangle set and cut out 28 triangles from the terracotta paste, then take the middle-sized triangle and cut out 28 triangles from the navy-blue paste (**B**).

2 Stick a navy-blue triangle inside each terracotta one, using sugar glue. Stick one triangle to each corner of the base tier and then arrange six triangles equally spaced between each of the corners. The exact space between the triangles will depend on the final dimensions of your cake

3 Place the set square up against the side of the cake centrally between two triangles. With the scriber, make a mark 2cm (¾in) up from the board (**C**). Make similar marks between all the triangles around the sides of the base cake.

## adding circles

1 Thinly roll out some terracotta and navy-blue modelling pastes then, using a no. 17 tube, cut out 14 circles of each colour (**D**). Attach these circles to the cake, using sugar glue, placing them over the scribed marks and alternating the colours.

### the gold scrolls

**1** Using a pencil, trace the scroll pattern on page 132 onto tracing or greaseproof paper. Cut the paper to the size of the template.

**2** Place the prepared template centrally on one side of the cake, checking that it is the correct way up. Secure in place with a few pins, then carefully scribe the pattern onto the cake by going over the pencil lines with either a scriber or pin. Remove all the pins and the template, and repeat for the remaining three sides.

### attaching the scrolls

**3** Dip a fine paintbrush into the sugar glue then paint over each scroll (**E**).

**4** Soften some of the antique-gold modelling paste and place in the sugar shaper with the small round disc and squeeze out a length.

*If the paste does not come out easily it is still too hard, so remove and re-soften.*

Place the length of paste over one of the painted glue scrolls and adjust its shape with a finger and/or a paintbrush (**F**). Cut the paste neatly at either end of the scroll with the tip of a small palette knife. Repeat for the remaining scrolls.

### the palmette motif

**1** Place the set square up against one side of the cake and scribe a vertical line above the central join of the scrolls, taking care not to touch the scrolls themselves (**G**).

**2** Thinly roll out some terracotta modelling paste between narrow spacers. Then, using the larger teardrop cutter set, cut four shapes using the largest teardrop cutter, and eight of each of the two smaller teardrop cutters.

**3** Thinly roll out some navy-blue modelling paste and cut eight shapes of each of the two smaller teardrop cutters, plus four of the middle-sized triangle.

### assembling the motif

**1** Arrange the cut-outs on your work board to resemble a radiating cluster of petals (**H**). Gently curve all but the central teardrop by fractionally reshaping the paste.

**2** Using sugar glue, stick the navy-blue triangles in position so that they rest on top of the central scrolls. Next, leaving a gap of 6mm (¼in) from the tip of the triangle, attach the largest teardrop vertically over the scribed line. Then attach the remaining teardrops in position.

**3** Finally, cut out a circle from the antique gold modelling paste using a no. 18 tube, and attach to the centre of the motif (**I**).

### corner motif

Cut four of the largest teardrop shapes from thinly rolled terracotta modelling paste and attach one vertically above each corner where the scrolls join. Cut out 12 teardrops from navy-blue modelling paste using the largest cutter from the small teardrop set. Curve them as shown in picture J, then stick in place. Cut antique-gold modelling paste circles using a no. 16 piping tube and stick one either side of each terracotta motif (**J**).

### top tile decoration

**1** Make a 15cm (6in) square template from a piece of greaseproof paper. Find the centre by folding it in half twice. Measure 4cm (1½in) from the centre of the square on each fold then, using these marks, draw an 8cm (3⅛in) square centrally on the template.

**2** Place the template on top of the cake and scribe the 8cm (3⅛in) square onto the cake. Thinly roll out some navy-blue modelling paste and

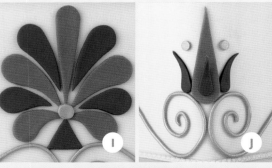

cut out an 8cm (3⅛in) square. Attach this to the cake on top of the scribed square. You want an exact fit, so straighten the edges as necessary with a smoother.

3 Mark the centre of the square and cut out a circle from antique-gold modelling paste, using the wider end of a piping tube, and place on top of the mark.

## creating the tile pattern

Add large terracotta and smaller antique gold teardrops to the tile to create the pattern (see right) then add embossing and trim around the tile (**K**) using the pastes and techniques described as for the main cake.

## finishing touches

1 Mix some edible antique gold dust with confectioners' glaze and use to paint over all the decorations made from the antique-gold modelling paste.

2 Using a non-toxic glue stick, attach the ribbons around the sides of the board to complete the cake.

# love the look

- Jazz up a plain cake with any of the decorative elements used here.
- The embosser can be used for decorating the cake board or the cake itself.
- Make a large scroll to decorate the sides of a plain cake.
- Use the tile decoration to top any plain, square cake.

# simple shortcuts

- Make the top tier only and place on a simply covered board.
- Simplify the top tile by just adding the cut-out teardrops without the trim.
- Use the triangle-and-dot pattern around the sides of the top tier as well as the lower tier and top with the tile.
- Omit the palmette pattern – the scrolls will still make an effective decoration for the top tier.

# small wonders

**Create Greek-inspired gifts that capture the essence of the art with these simple but evocative cake 'boxes'.**
Cut a cake into portions 4cm (1½in) square x 3.5cm (1⅜in) high. Then cover each portion with light-gold sugarpaste.
Create the decoration as for the main cake but using the small teardrop cutter set to create the patterns and the smallest cutter from the equilateral triangle set. You can use the navy-blue embossed trim topped with gold for some of the bases and a cream or gold embossed band for others.

# nursery christening bricks

A stack of decorated bricks makes a delightful cake for a baby's christening and is great fun to make. The cake is made from four, decorated pastel-coloured cubes. You can go to town with your choice of suitable motifs, choosing either pictures made using the simple templates provided in the book, bought cutters or your own designs. What makes the cake so striking is that some of the motifs are made using different coloured pastes so that each motif contains details in several colours – a simple but professional touch. Perfectly small mini-cake bricks (see below and page 89) accompany the cake.

### Or make this cake for ...
• baby's first or second birthday • an older child – simply choose suitable decorations, such as brightly coloured geometric shapes, space ships, flowers or cut-out fairies. The colours you choose will also completely transform the cake.

# you will need...

## materials

- sugarpaste (rolled fondant):
  1.3kg (2lb 14oz) orange
  400g (14oz) yellow
  350g (12oz) purple
  175g (6oz) lilac
  150g (5oz) light pink
  450g (1lb) coral pink
  175g (6oz) dark pink
  350g (12oz) lime green
  150g (5oz) light aqua
  350g (12oz) mid blue
  50g (2oz) brown
  50g (2oz) white

- icing (confectioners') sugar (optional)

- white vegetable fat (shortening)

- cakes: four 10cm (4in) cube cakes (cut a 10cm (4in) deep × 20cm (8in) square cake into quarters or make two 20cm (8in) shallower cakes and stack them to produce the required depth) (see pages 8–11)

- buttercream, or apricot glaze and marzipan (see pages 16–17)

- clear spirit, such as gin or vodka (if using fruit cake)

- gum tragacanth

- sugar glue (see page 14)

- ½ quantity of royal icing

## equipment

- 5mm (³⁄₁₆in) spacers

- 30cm (12in) square cake drum (board)

- smoother

- palette knife

- set square

- spirit level (optional)

- four 10cm (4in) hardboard cake boards

- waxed paper

- small, sharp scissors

- patchwork cutters: baby lion, large daisies, nursery set (rabbit and giraffe toys), train, butterflies, unicorn, Make A Cradle (small teddy for socks)

- narrow spacers made from 1.5mm (¹⁄₁₆in) thick card

- multi-ribbon cutter (FMM)

- craft knife

- card or stiff plastic, such as a milk carton

- a selection of plain round piping tubes (tips)

- cutters: flat floral collection sets 1 and 2 (LC) or similar, elegant hearts (LC) or similar, stylish stars (LC) or similar, starburst and simple snowflakes (LC), large flat flora set (LC)

- dowels

- coral-pink ribbon and non-toxic glue stick

# preparation

### covering the board

Knead 1kg (2¼lb) of orange sugarpaste to warm it and make it more pliable then roll out between 5mm (³⁄₁₆in) spacers using icing sugar or white vegetable fat to prevent sticking. Lift up the paste, using a rolling pin for support, and place it over the board. Take a smoother and, using a circular motion, smooth the paste to give a level surface. Using a palette knife, trim the edges flush with the sides of the board, taking care to keep the cut vertical and the corners sharp. Place to one side to dry.

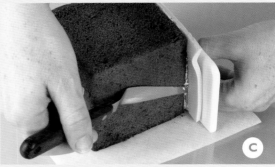

A

B

C

D

E

F

G

# stage one

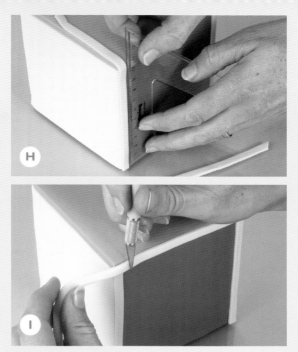

## preparing the cakes for covering

**Sponge cakes** Take a large knife and level the top of each sponge cake, then adjust the sides so that they are all vertical and the corners square (**A**).
**Fruit cakes** Turn the cake(s) upside down, so that the flat surface is uppermost. Ensure the top is horizontal and adjust the height of one side if necessary by adding marzipan under the base. Trim the sides of the cakes, if necessary, so that they are vertical and the corners square.

*It is worthwhile spending time getting this right, as the shape of the cakes is fundamental to the design.*

## covering the cubes

1 Stick the cakes to the hardboard cake boards, using apricot glaze or buttercream as appropriate, and then place onto waxed paper.

2 If using a fruit cake, cover with apricot glaze and marzipan, keeping the corners sharp; follow directions for sugarpaste below.

3 Knead 150g (5oz) of orange sugarpaste until warm. Then roll the paste between 5mm (³/₁₆in) spacers, using icing sugar or white vegetable fat to prevent sticking. Cut one edge straight, using a palette knife.

4 To help the sugarpaste stick to the cake, cover with a thin layer of buttercream (for a sponge cake) or paint over the marzipan with clear spirit (for a fruit cake). Lift up the sugarpaste and position it over the side of the cake placing the straight edge against the lower edge of the cake (**B**). Smooth the paste to give an even surface.

## fitting the paste and embossing

1 Roughly cut away the excess paste with a pair of scissors. (**Note:** you are just removing the excess weight not trying to give a neat finish.) Place the smoother onto the surface of the sugarpaste so that it slightly overhangs the edge of the cake then, using a palette knife, remove the excess paste by cutting away from the cake onto the smoother (**C**).

2 Take the baby lion cutter and press it centrally into the soft sugarpaste and remove to leave an embossed shape (**D**).

3 Cover the opposite side of the cube in the same way, using 150g (5oz) yellow sugarpaste and a different cutter.

## covering the remaining sides

1 For the next side, roll out 150g (5oz) of another coloured sugarpaste, cut one edge straight then make a cut at right angles. Position the sugarpaste on the cake as for the first side so that the edge abuts one side of the orange square (**E**).

2 Trim as for the first side then straighten the corner with a smoother. Repeat for the remaining side, using a different coloured paste.

## the top

Knead and roll out another 150g (5oz) of sugarpaste. Use to cover the top of the cake, cutting to shape in exactly the same way as before. This time you will have to cut upwards against the smoother (**F**).

## the remaining cakes

Cover the remaining cakes with the different-coloured sugarpastes, embossing some of the sides with the suggested cutters but leaving other sides blank. The tops of each cube are not embossed.

## making modelling paste

Take 50g (2oz) of each of the coloured sugarpastes and knead in 1.5ml (¼ tsp) gum tragacanth to each colour to make modelling paste. Leave the paste to mature, ideally overnight.

# stage two

## adding border decoration

1 Choose a colour of modelling paste and knead the paste to warm it. If the paste is either a bit hard or too crumbly add a little white fat and/or boiled water to soften. It should be firm with some elasticity.

2 Roll out the paste between the narrow spacers. Set the multi-ribbon cutter to a width of 8mm (⁵/₁₆in) then use to cut two ribbons (**G**).

3 Paint glue along the vertical cut edges of the sugarpaste on one side of a cube and position the strips on top of the glue to disguise the cut edge. Check that the strips are vertical using a set square (**H**) then cut to fit with a craft knife.

4 Cut more strips with the multiribbon cutter in different colours, and use to disguise the edges of the paste on all of the bricks, each time cutting to fit with a craft knife (**I**).

# decorating the embossed motifs

1 Add colour to the embossed sides following the technique described for the train below:

**For the train** roll out some lime-green, brown and mid-blue modelling paste between the narrow spacers. Press the train cutter into the lime-green paste. Cut out the main shapes of the train as shown in picture K; use a craft knife held vertically to cut along the embossed lines of the shapes (**J**). Press the cutter into the different coloured pastes and cut out the following shapes: wheels and funnel from the brown paste, and the trim from the blue. Next, attach the modelling-paste pieces to their embossed positions on the cake using sugar glue (**K**).

2 Repeat for the other embossed motifs with either your choice of colours or by using the pictures to guide you.

# adding designs using templates

You can add your own designs to the cake; just find suitable pictures from magazines or the Internet, reduce or enlarge them to a suitable size and make templates. Then follow the instructions for the socks below, adapting them as appropriate:

## socks

1 Transfer the template on page 133 onto card or stiff plastic such as a milk carton. Thinly roll out some lilac modelling paste between narrow spacers. Place the template on the paste and cut around it with a craft knife. Repeat to make two (**L**).

2 Cut the template along the lines and place the heel, toe and top sections on purple paste. Cut around these with a craft knife and then place in position on top of the lilac socks.

3 Using the small teddy embosser from the Make A Cradle set, add a yellow teddy head to each sock (**M**). Remove the teddy's eyes using a small piping tube and attach in place on a cake (**N**).

## other templates

Templates for a bib and rattle can be found on page 133. Create these in the same way as the socks, selecting appropriate colours to match your cakes (**O**).

## simple cutter designs

These are ideal if you are a little short of time. Use whatever cutters you have – flowers, stars, snowflakes, hearts, and so on (see Small Wonders cakes, opposite). Cut shapes from thinly rolled modelling paste and attach to the cakes using sugar glue.

## stacking the cakes

Place two cakes on the covered cake board, referring to the finished pictures for placement. Dowel (see page 22) the two inner corners of these cakes, using a 10cm (4in) square paper template to help with placement, and dowel the cake that will be placed on top of them. Attach this cake in place using a little royal icing to secure and referring to the main picture for guidance. Finally, place the top cake in position.

## finishing touches

Using a non-toxic glue stick attach the ribbon around the sides of the board to complete the cake.

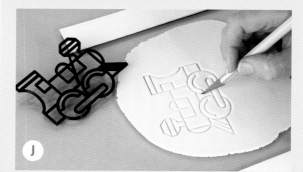

J

K

L

M

N

O

## love the look

- Use the decoration suggestions to decorate a round or square cake that you have covered in sugarpaste in a pastel shade.
- Cover the sides of a large square cake (or two stacked and trimmed cakes), trim the edges and decorate with cut-outs of your choice suitable for any occasion.
- Cutters make useful embossers for all kinds of decoration schemes.

## simple shortcuts

- For a quick but just as attractive finish, leave the embossed decorations made using the cutters on the sides of the cake without decorating them.
- Cut a shop-bought square cake into cubes and decorate as here.
- Leave more sides plain.
- Use simple cut-out shapes for all the sides.
- Make the trims in the same colour for all the cubes.

# small wonders

**Make these baby-sized bricks in their pastel shades decorated to scale, as gifts for the young at heart.**

Cut a cake into 5cm (2in) cube portions. Then cover each portion as for the main cake, embossing some of the sides of the cubes with suitable embossers, such as patchwork cutters: polar bears, nursery set, daisy chain, elephants, nursery items, and butterflies. Cover the cut edges with strips of paste as before and add a few simple cut-outs of hearts and flowers, and so on, to the remaining faces.

# op art boxes

This stunning and eye-catching creation captures the 1960s when bold black-and-white designs, called Op Art, took the fashion and interior design worlds by storm. These smart and sophisticated Op Art Boxes are stacked irregularly with some faces plain and others decorated with the contrasting themes of flat floral patterns and geometric shapes. This cake would make an ideal gift for anyone with an eye for style or for someone who loves the 1960s. The decoration is surprisingly straightforward to make – just be careful to keep the stripes straight. Make a smart mini-cake (see below and page 95) with the same designs scaled down for the perfect retro gift.

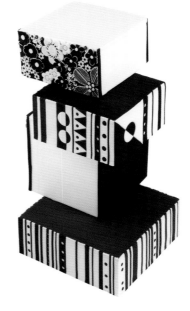

## or make this cake for …
• an art student.• someone who was a style slave in the 1960s. • a wedding cake for a couple who love everything retro.

# you will need ...

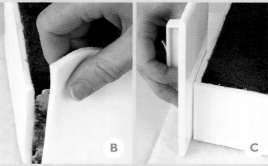

## materials

- sugarpaste (rolled fondant): 3kg (6lb 10oz) white, 1.5kg (3lb 5oz) black
- icing (confectioners') sugar (optional)
- white vegetable fat
- cakes: four 15cm (6in) square, one 20cm (8in) square (see pages 8–12)
- buttercream, or apricot glaze and marzipan (see pages 16–17)
- clear spirit, such as gin or vodka (if using fruit cake)
- modelling paste: 225g (8oz) black, 225g (8oz) white
- sugar glue (see page 14)
- 1/4 quantity of royal icing

## equipment

- 5mm (³/₁₆in) spacers
- 35.5cm (14in) square cake drum (board)
- smoother
- palette knife
- waxed paper
- small, sharp scissors
- set square and spirit level (optional)
- three 15cm (6in) square hardboard cake boards
- straightedge
- narrow spacers made from 1.5mm (¹/₁₆in) thick card
- craft knife
- piping tubes (tips), nos 18, 16, 4, 2 (PME)
- 5cm (2in) diamond cutter (LC)
- circle cutters: 2.5cm (1in) and 3.3cm (1¼in) (FMM Geometric set)
- clear plastic, such as a plastic bag
- flower cutters: 3.5cm (1³/₈in) rose petal cutter, large blossom cutters (FMM), small plunger blossom cutters (PME), flat floral collection set 1(LC), 4.5cm (1¾in) dorsal sepal from moth orchid cutter set (LC), or similar
- multi-ribbon cutter
- dowels
- black ribbon with white spots and non-toxic glue stick

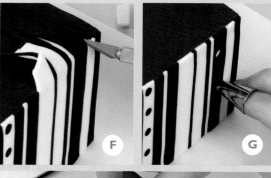

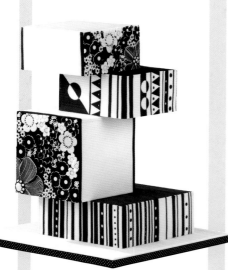

# preparation

## covering the board

Knead 1.1kg (2½lb) of white sugarpaste to warm it and make it more pliable, then roll out between 5mm (3/16 in) spacers using icing sugar or white vegetable fat to prevent sticking. Lift up the paste place over the cake drum. Use a smoother to smooth the paste level. Trim the edges flush with the sides of the board using a palette knife.

# stage one

## preparing the cakes for covering

**Sponge cakes** Take a large knife and level the top of each sponge cake, then adjust the sides so that they are all vertical and the corners square.

**Fruit cakes** Turn the cake(s) upside down, so that the flat surface is uppermost. Ensure the top is horizontal. Trim the sides of the cakes, if necessary, so that they are vertical and the corners square.

## covering the base-tier sides

1 Place the 20cm (8in) cake on waxed paper. If using a fruit cake cover with apricot glaze and marzipan, follow directions for sugarpaste.

2 Knead 500g (1lb 2oz) of white sugarpaste until warm. Roll the paste between 5mm (³/₁₆in) spacers to a length of 25.5cm (10in) and wide enough to cover two cake sides when cut lengthways. Cut the paste in half lengthways.

3 To help the sugarpaste stick to the cake, cover with a thin layer of buttercream (for a sponge cake) or paint over the marzipan with clear spirit (for a fruit cake).

4 Lift up one half of the sugarpaste, using a rolling pin for support, and position over the side of the cake, placing the straight edge against the lower edge of the cake. Take a smoother and smooth the paste. Roughly cut away the excess paste with a pair of scissors. (**Note:** you are just removing the excess weight not trying to give a neat finish.)

5 Place the smoother onto the surface of the sugarpaste so that it slightly overhangs the edge of the cake. Using a palette knife, remove the excess paste by cutting away from the cake onto the smoother (**A**).

6 For the second side, make a cut at right angles to the straight edge of the remaining sugarpaste then position the sugarpaste on the cake so that the edges abut (**B**). Trim as for the first side, then straighten the corner with a smoother (**C**). Repeat for the remaining sides.

## covering the base-tier top

Knead and roll out 700g (1½lb) of black sugarpaste. Use to cover the top of the cake, cutting to shape in exactly the same way, although this time you will have to cut upwards against the smoother (**D**).

## covering the cube cake

1 Stack two of the 15cm (6in) cakes to form a cube using either buttercream or apricot glaze, then place the stacked cakes onto one of the hardboard cake boards and position on waxed paper.

2 Cover using 500g (1b 2oz) of sugarpaste for each side (two sides are black and two white; the top is white).

3 Place the remaining cakes on the 15cm (6in) cake boards. Using sugarpaste, cover the cakes as follows:
**Third tier** White sides and black top.
**Top tier** Two white sides, two black sides and a white top.

# stage two

## decorating the striped base tier

1 Thinly roll out some black and white modelling paste between narrow spacers, cut one edge of each colour straight then, using a set square and a craft knife, cut strips of varying thicknesses from each colour (**E**).

2 Paint over part of one side of the cake with sugar glue and place the first vertical strip in position at one corner, draping the excess paste over the top of the cake. Add a second strip in the contrasting colour and continue until about a third of the side is covered. Next take a craft knife and, holding it horizontally, carefully remove the excess paste from the top of the cake (**F**).

## making dots

Create dots in some of the stripes by removing circles using the suggested piping tubes (**G**). Replace the circles in the white stripes with black ones cut from thinly rolled paste using the same size tube. Continue until all the sides of the cake are covered.

## upper striped tier

1 Add the stripes and small dots to the upper tier as for the base tier. To create the zigzag pattern, cut long diamonds from black and white pastes rolled out between the narrow spacers. Cut each in half to create triangles (**H**), then attach to the cake to create the vertical zigzag pattern.

2 To create the large square, measure the height of the cake and make a square paper template with sides the same length. Fold the square in half diagonally and then cut in two along the fold. Using the triangle templates cut out modelling paste triangles from the black and white pastes and attach to the side of the cake to form a square. Take the 3.3cm (1¼in) circle cutter and carefully remove the paste from the centre of the square. Reposition the half circles in the opposite sections.

## making the circles

To create the large circles within the stripes, firstly remove the circles from the decorated cake using a 2.5cm (1in) circle cutter placed partly over the black and white stripes. Cut some fresh circles from the black and white pastes and, using the removed sections as templates, cut the circle sections in the opposite shade to those that have been removed. Attach in place.

### small flower cake

1 To make the stripy flowers, very thinly roll out some black and white modelling paste.

2 Cut out similar-sized rectangles, such as 7.5 x 2.5cm (3 x 1in). Stack the rectangles on top of each other, alternating the shades. Roll across the top of the pile to secure and thin the paste a fraction. Place a ruler lengthways on top of the stack and, using a craft knife, cut through the stack to create a straight edge. Then repeat at 3mm (³/₃₂in) intervals to create strips (**I**). Place the strips under plastic to prevent them drying out.

### making stripy petals

1 Take two strips and place them side by side between narrow spacers. Roll along the strips to lengthen and thin the paste (**J**). Cut four petals using the rose petal cutter, then widen the top of each petal by rolling a rolling pin over the petal in a radial movement, pressing down more firmly at the top. The result can be seen in the picture (**K**). Place the prepared petals under plastic.

2 Thinly roll out the white modelling paste, place a prepared petal on the paste and briefly roll to stick. Roughly cut around the petal with a craft knife and then trim the paste very close to the petal with scissors (**L**). Repeat for the remaining petals.

### the flower centre

Attach the petals to the cake using sugar glue (see the main picture for placement). For the flower centre, cut some white circles using the no. 16 tube. Press these circles onto thinly rolled black paste and then cut out larger circles using a no. 18 tube. Place the circles in the centre of the flower.

### white flowers

1 Roll out some white modelling paste and cut out one large and three small flowers using the large and small blossom cutters.

2 Emboss the centre of the smaller ones with the end of a no. 18 piping tube, then place a no. 4 tube on the end of your finger and remove a ring of circles around the embossed circle (**M**). Finally, move each petal slightly in a clockwise direction around its centre to elongate the small circles.

3 Emboss the centre of the larger flowers with the wide end of a piping tube and remove a ring of circles using firstly a no. 2 tube and then a no. 2 (see main picture). Move each petal clockwise as before to create a spiral centre. Attach to the cake with sugar glue.

### black flowers

1 Roll out some white modelling paste and cut out five flowers using the five-petal flat floral cutter.

2 Place a smoother over the flowers and press down on the paste to enlarge them fractionally.

3 Cut out five of the same flower shape from thinly rolled black paste and allow the paste to harden for a few minutes. Paint sugar glue over the white flowers then, using a palette knife, lift the black flowers and place them carefully over the white so that a rim of white shows around the black (**N**).

4 Attach the flowers to the cake using sugar glue, referring to the picture for placement. Add some flower centres, using circles cut with a no. 16 tube.

### eight-petal flowers

Make four eight-petal flowers, in the same way as above, using the eight-petal flat floral cutter. Attach to the cake with sugar glue, overlapping the flowers in places to give a more textured look. Add some white centres cut from modelling paste using a no. 18 piping tube.

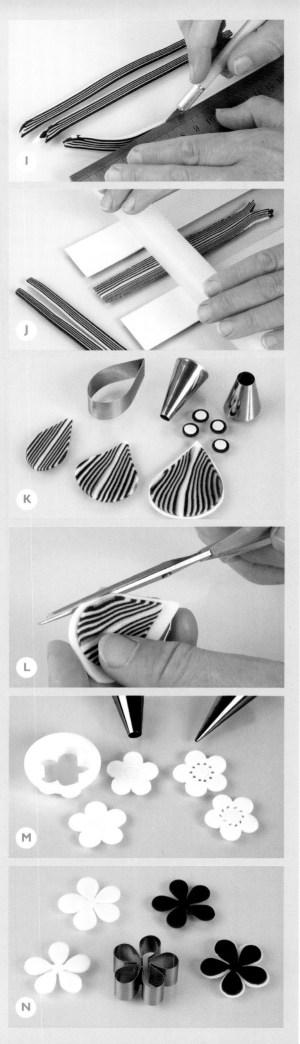

## trimming the edges

Where the flowers overlap the edges of the cake, cut away the excess paste using a craft knife.

## small blossoms

**1** Thinly roll out some black and white modelling paste and cut out white small, six-petal blossoms using the smallest cutter from the flat floral collection and white five-petal blossoms using the small blossom plunger set or similar.

**2** Using a no. 4 tube, cut black circles. Add these to the centres of the six-petal blossoms. For the white blossom remove the centre of each flower with a no. 2 tube. Cut a few black blossoms using the smallest plunger cutter and add a white centre to each.

**3** Attach the blossoms to the cake, referring to the picture.

## decorating the cube cake

Create the decoration for this cake as for the small flower cake but make a large stripy flower using the dorsal sepal cutter from the moth orchid cutter set. For the centre use a flattened ball of white modelling paste and add small circles.

## finishing touches

Attach the ribbon around the side of the cake drum. Thinly roll out some black and white modelling paste between narrow spacers. Set the multi-ribbon cutter to 7mm (⁹/₃₂in) and cut out strips of each colour. Attach over the edges of the flower cube.

## stacking the cakes

Dowel the cakes (see page 00), referring to the main picture for dowel placement. Place the base cake 5cm (2in) from two sides of the board (not centrally). Attach with royal icing. Stack the remaining cakes using royal icing to secure (see main picture).

# love the look

• Use the stripy flower to make a simply iced cake look fabulous. You could use toning colours instead of black and white.
• Cover a plain, iced cake with a variety of cut-out flowers. Even a few flowers in a flowing line across the cake will make a striking effect but will be quick and easy to do.
• Jazz up a bought square cake with the stripy design.

# simple shortcuts

• Any square cake can be decorated in either the stripy design or the floral design for a smaller but equally as dramatic cake.
• Simplify the geometric design to just stripes, without the circles or triangles for a quicker cake.
• Make a two-tiered stripy cake – ideal for someone who likes cake decoration that is simple and stylish.

# small wonders

**Great things come in small boxes, so if you like your cakes neat and small, these stylish mini-cakes are just as striking as the main cake.**

Cut the cake into 5cm (2in) squares × 3.5cm (1³/₈in) deep. Then cover and decorate each portion as for the main cakes. Scale down the designs and simplify them by using mostly plain stripes and adding just one or two stripes with dots cut out using small piping tubes. Choose the smallest flowers from the main cake with just one or two accent flowers in black on white using the five-petal flat floral cutter and the eight-petal flat floral cutter.

# eastern ornament

Reproduce the exotic beauty of Indian decoration by creating this hexagonal stacked cake with its ornate separator and wired topper. Although a wedding cake is not a customary part of Asian wedding celebrations, cakes like this one are growing in popularity. Here, the traditional Indian red and burgundy colours combine with paisley and Mughal arches, and the cake glistens with opulent gold details. Although the designs are intricate, they are mostly created using cutters, and you could easily simplify the cake and still achieve a splendid result. Fascinating little Indian-jewelled mini-cake 'boxes' (below and on page 103) add that final, luxurious touch.

### Or make this cake for …
• anyone who loves India, its art and culture • a wedding cake for a couple who love to travel • someone who loves ornamentation and the extraordinary.

# you will need...

## materials

- sugarpaste (rolled fondant): 2.6kg (5lb 12oz) ivory, 2kg (4½lb) burgundy

- icing (confectioners') sugar (optional)

- white vegetable fat (shortening)

- cakes: 30cm (12in) side-to-side hexagonal, 23cm (9in) round, 15cm (6in) side-to-side hexagonal (pages 8–12)

- buttercream, or apricot glaze and marzipan (see pages 16–17)

- modelling paste: 100g (3½oz) red, 125g (4½oz) gold, 150g (5oz) cream, 50g (2oz) ivory, 75g (3oz) burgundy

- sugar glue (see page 14)

- 1 quantity of royal icing

- gold edible dust

- confectioners' glaze

- paste colours: ivory or cream

- sugar balls: 4mm (⅛in) silver, 4mm (⅛in) pearlised gold

## for the topper

- posy pick

- oasis fix

- 2mm (14 SWG/12 AWG) deep red aluminium wire

- jewellery pliers

- 28 gauge gold binding/beading wire

- a selection of beads to match the cake; Lindy used:
  4 × 12mm (¹⁵⁄₃₂in) gold pearls
  2 × 8mm (⁵⁄₁₆in) gold pearls
  2 × 12mm (¹⁵⁄₃₂in) ivory pearls
  4 × 8mm (¹⁵⁄₁₆in) ivory pearls
  3 × 12mm (¹⁵⁄₃₂in) silver pearls
  3 × 8mm (⁵⁄₁₆in) silver pearls

- invisible/clear thread

- masking tape

## equipment

- cake drums (boards): 40.5cm (16in) and 23cm (9in) round

- gold 'S' with scrolls cake separator (LC)

- glass-headed dressmakers' pins

- 5mm (³⁄₁₆in) spacers

- smoother

- palette knife

- small embossers: Indian style (HP set 10, flower embroidery), flower motif (HP set 1, small floral)

- hardboard cake boards: 30cm (12in), 23cm (9in) and 15cm (6in) round

- waxed paper

- set square

- scriber (optional)

- cutters: Mughal arch (LC), Indian scrolls and petal set (LC), large teardrop cutters, (LC), paisley cutters (LC), small teardrop cutters (LC), small six-petal flower cutter, such as one from flat floral collection set 1 (LC), 7cm (2¾in) circle cutter

- narrow spacers made from 1.5mm (¹⁄₁₆in) thick card

- multi-ribbon cutter (FMM)

- Dresden tool

- sugar shaper with small and medium round discs

- cutting wheel

- paintbrush

- craft knife

- fluting tool (JEM, no. 2 tool)

- dowels

- 13cm (5in) round cake card

- piping tubes (tips): nos 18, 17, 4, 2, 1

- reusable piping bag and coupler

- burgundy ribbon and non-toxic glue stick

- 13cm (5in) circle of non-slip matting

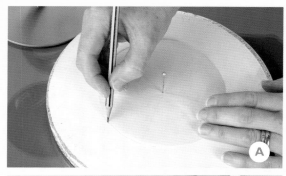

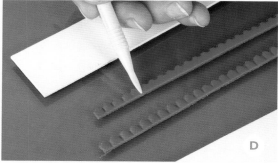

# preparation

## covering the boards

1 To mark the separator position on the base of the 23cm (9in) round cake drum, make two paper circles, one by drawing around the board and one by drawing around the separator's base plate. Fold the circles in half and in half again to find their centres. Place the 23cm (9in) circle on the underside of the drum and mark the drum's centre with a glass-headed pin. Remove the larger circle and replace with the smaller. Draw lightly around the edge to mark its position (**A**). Remove and replace with the separator, then draw around its base with a pencil. Keep the templates.

2 Using 600g (1lb 5oz) of ivory sugarpaste, cover the 23cm (9in) cake drum and trim the edges (see page 16).

3 Position the smoother vertically against the edge of the board then place the Indian-style embosser against the smoother and press it into the soft paste. Line up the embosser so that the next shape will be adjacent to the first and press down (**B**). Continue making this pattern all around the edge of the board.

4 Cover the 40.5cm (16in) drum with ivory paste and emboss as before. Leave both drums to dry.

## stage one

### covering the large hexagonal cake

Place the cake on the 30cm (12in) round hardboard cake board then place on waxed paper. Cover with buttercream or apricot glaze and marzipan. Use 1.5kg (3lb 5oz) of the burgundy sugarpaste to cover the cake. Smooth the surface and trim away the excess paste (see page 18).

### covering the small hexagonal cake

Place the cake on the 15cm (6in) round hardboard cake board, and then place it on waxed paper. Cover the cake with buttercream or apricot glaze and marzipan then cover with the remaining burgundy sugarpaste.

### marking the arch

Find the central point at the base of one side of the cake. Place the set square up against the cake at this point and make a mark 7cm (2¾in) above the base, using a scriber or glass-headed pin. Repeat for the other sides. Take the Mughal arch cutter and position the pointed top of the arch onto the scribed mark. Adjust the placement of the cutter to ensure the arch is level. Carefully emboss the arch into the soft sugarpaste. Repeat for the other sides.

### covering the round cake

Place the cake onto the 23cm (9in) round hardboard and then place on waxed paper. Cover the cake with the remaining ivory sugarpaste. Set the cakes aside to dry.

## stage two

Carefully transfer the large hexagonal cake to the prepared board.

### making the trim for the large cake

1 Knead the red modelling paste and then roll it out into a long strip between narrow spacers. Take the multi-ribbon cutter and, using one cutting wheel and one wavy-line cutting wheel, set the distance between the two outside edges to 7mm (9/32in). Cut strips of red paste (**C**).

2 Indent the strips with the sharp end of a Dresden tool, as shown (**D**). Paint sugar glue around the base of the cake and add the textured strips, abutting them together.

3 Soften some gold modelling paste by kneading in some white vegetable fat and boiled water until the consistency of chewing gum. Put into the sugar shaper, with the small round disc, and squeeze out a length. Place the length around the base of the cake. Cut to size and secure with sugar glue.

### the side decoration

1 To create the central red section, roll out the red modelling paste between the narrow spacers. Cut out six shapes using the Indian petal cutter. Using the cutting wheel, emboss eight curved lines over the shapes (see picture E for placement). Using a thin paintbrush, paint glue over the embossed lines.

2 Squeeze out eight short lengths for each petal using cream modelling paste from the sugar shaper fitted with the small round disc. Place them over the embossed curved lines. Cut to size. Insert the pointed end of the fluting tool into the paste where the curves cross, to reveal the red paste below (**E**).

## paisley and teardrops

1 Thinly roll out some of the gold, cream, ivory and burgundy modelling pastes and cut out the following shapes:

**Gold** Six of the largest teardrop from the large set; 12 of the largest paisley (six using each cutting edge).
**Cream** 12 of the middle teardrop; 12 of the smallest teardrop from the large set; 12 of the larger Indian scroll (six with each cutting edge).
**Ivory** 12 of the second largest paisley (six with each cutting edge); 12 of the smallest; 12 of the middle teardrop from the teardrop set.
**Burgundy** 12 of each of the two smallest paisley shapes (six with each cutting edge).

2 Take the large, gold teardrops and remove their centres with the largest cutter from the smaller set. Attach the burgundy paisley shapes and ivory teardrops to the larger shapes, as shown (**F**).

3 Paint sugar glue around the outside of the burgundy paisley on top of the ivory one. Using the paste in the sugar shaper, squeeze out lengths and place on top of the glue (**G**). Cut neatly to fit at the point of the shape with a craft knife.

## attaching the shapes

1 Find the central point at the base of one side of the cake. Place the set square against the cake at this point and scribe a short vertical line above the trim. Make a mark at a height of 7.7cm (3¹/₃₂in) above the base. Repeat for the other sides.

2 Using sugar glue, attach the teardrops in place, positioning the largest so that its top just covers the 7.7cm (3¹/₃₂in) mark (see H). Add the ivory paisleys underneath then centrally position the prepared red petal so that its tip curves outwards. Add the gold paisley shapes so that they sit above the trim. Overlap the red centre. Add the cream Indian scrolls.

3 Take the head of a glass-headed pin and indent it into the centres of the ivory teardrops and the smaller burgundy paisleys (**H**).

## stacking the cakes

Dowel the large, hexagonal cake (see page 22) and the round cake. Using royal icing, attach the round cake centrally on top of the hexagonal cake.

## adding trim to the round cake

1 Using the circular paper templates made earlier, find the centre of the cake and then mark the position of the separator by scribing around the smaller template. Position the 13cm (5in) cake card within the scribed circle and paint a line of sugar glue onto the cake around the card.

2 Roll out a strip of red modelling paste and cut the trim as for the base tier, using the multi-ribbon cutter. Texture as before and place in position around the card. Cut to fit. Remove the card.

3 Squeeze some gold modelling paste from the sugar shaper with the medium round disc and place around the base of the cake. Cut to size and secure with sugar glue.

4 Thinly roll out the cream modelling paste between narrow spacers and cut out 45–50 of the small Indian scrolls (**I**). Using sugar glue to stick the shapes in place, arrange these on top of the base tier, abutting the gold trim (see picture K).

## paisley decoration

There are four different paisley patterns decorating this tier, which are grouped in pairs according to their size:

## paisley 1

1 Roll out burgundy, cream and red modelling pastes. Cut ten large burgundy paisleys, ten of the second smallest cream and ten of the small red (for each, cut five with each cutting edge).

**F**

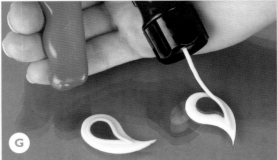
**G**

**H**

**I**

**J**

**2** Stack the shapes as shown (**J**) and attach, evenly distributing them. Indent the centre of each with the pin. Dip a fine paintbrush into the sugar glue and paint around one of the paisley shapes, extending the point into a scroll.

**3** Squeeze out a length of gold modelling paste from the sugar shaper with the small round disc.

**4** Place the length over the glue (**K**) and adjust the scroll. Cut the paste at the end of the scroll with the tip of a small palette knife. Repeat for the other paisley shapes.

## paisley 2

Cut ten large red paisleys, ten of the second smallest gold paisleys and ten circles using the no. 18 piping tube. Assemble them as before and attach to the cake, as shown (**L**). Add trim and scrolls using burgundy paste.

## paisleys 3 and 4

Use the second largest paisley cutters to cut out the background shapes. Make about seven pairs – the exact number will depend on how your previous pairs have been placed. Cut out the shapes, referring to the pictures, and attach to the cake in the spaces, leaving enough room for the scrolls. Add the scrolls.

## floral detail

Thinly roll out the gold modelling paste between the narrow spacers and cut out 20 small six-petal flowers. Place on waxed paper. Mix the edible gold dust with confectioners' glaze and paint over each one (**M**). Allow the glaze to set (1–2 minutes) then remove the centre from each flower with the no. 18 piping tube (**N**). Attach two flowers, one above and one below each large paisley pair (see picture L).

## decorating the small hexagonal cake

Carefully transfer the cake to the prepared board.

## the side decoration

**1** Roll out some cream modelling paste between narrow spacers. Press the arch cutter into the paste, leaving enough paste above and to the sides of the arch to cut out the required shape.

**2** Using a set square and craft knife, cut across the base of the arch (**O**). then cut the sides at 90 degrees to the base. Cut away the top 7mm ($^9/_{32}$in) of the arch. Leave to harden slightly and make five more.

**3** Using the embossed arches on the cake as a guide, stick the prepared arches in position.

## trimming the arches

**1** Squeeze some gold modelling paste from the sugar shaper with the medium round disc. Place around the sides and top edge of an arch. Cut to size and secure with sugar glue. Repeat for the other arches.

**2** Squeeze some ivory modelling paste from the sugar shaper with the small round disc and place it around the sides and top of the arch.

## the columns

**1** Make six columns for the arches from thinly rolled ivory modelling paste 12mm x 2.5cm ($^{15}/_{32}$ x 1in) and attach in place. Add gold rectangles to fill the gap between the arch and column. Stick in place and cut each end at an angle. Add additional trim as desired.

**2** Cut six small teardrops from red paste and attach them to the top of each arch. Roll six pea-sized balls of gold modelling paste and attach them to the cake so that they join the arches together. Flatten each ball slightly and emboss with the small flower motif (**P**).

## the top decoration

1 Insert the posy pick into the centre of the cake so that its top lies flush with the top of the sugarpaste covering.

2 Thinly roll out some ivory modelling paste and cut out a 7cm (2¾in) circle. Find the centre using a paper template then, using the no. 18 piping tube, cut a circle from the centre (**Q**). Allow the paste to harden slightly before placing the circle centrally on top of the cake, lining up the hole with the posy pick.

3 Squeeze some gold modelling paste from the sugar shaper with the medium round disc and place it around the ivory circle.

4 Thinly roll out the cream modelling paste and cut out 14 of the small Indian scrolls. Use sugar glue to stick the shapes in place around the circle abutting the gold trim (see cake opposite).

5 Cut small circles from thinly rolled red modelling paste using a no. 4 tube (**R**) and add one to each scroll. Add one to each of the scrolls on top of the base tier.

## royal iced detail

1 To pipe the dots, colour the royal icing ivory or a very pale cream. Check the consistency and adjust as necessary, by adding more sugar or boiled water (you need to pipe round dots not pointed cones).

2 Use the coupler and piping bag, and no. 2 tube. Half-fill with royal icing and pipe dots on the paisley tier (**S**). Change the tube to a no. 1 and pipe dots around the shapes and patterns on the cake (see finished cake for reference).

*If some of your dots are slightly pointed, quickly knock the point back into the dot with a damp brush before the icing sets to create a rounded edge.*

## the topper

1 Place some oasis fix into the posy pick. Cut six 33cm (13in) and three 38cm (15in) lengths of the deep-red aluminium wire. Clasp the end of one length with pliers and bend to create a loose coil, referring to the template on page 134 (**T**) Bend the other end of the wire at a point 3cm (1⅛in) from the end, to allow it to sit correctly in the posy pick. Make three of each shape.

2 Insert the shorter lengths in pairs into the posy pick to line up with the top of three arches. Insert the remaining wires between these to create the top of the wire design. Bind the crossover point with the gold binding/beading wire.

3 Thread and knot two 12mm (¹⁵⁄₃₂in) gold pearls to either end of a length of clear thread. Then drape the thread over the top of the bound wires at the crossover point. Repeat using 8mm (⁵⁄₁₆in) ivory pearls.

# stage three

## finishing touches

1 Add sugar balls, using royal icing to secure, to all the circular indentations made in the teardrop and paisley shapes (these balls can tarnish quickly so add them to the shapes at the last minute).

2 Attach the ribbon around the sides of the two cake drums.

## assembling the cake and adding beads

1 Attach the separator to the cake (see page 23). Thread and knot a selection of beads onto clear thread and attach to hang at varying heights around the top plate of the separator using masking tape to secure in place.

2 Place the non-slip matting on the top plate of the separator and position the top tier to line up with the drawn circle on the drum. Ensure the sides of the top cake line up with those on the base.

# love the look ...

- Use the splendid cut-out detail from the base layer to decorate a one-tier cake.
- The paisley shapes and golden flowers give an exotic touch to any cake.
- Add the border trim to brighten up a cake and board.

## simple shortcuts

- Make the top tier with its wired topper as a stunning cake for a smaller celebration.
- Make fewer decorations for the centre tier, or even make this tier plain.
- Make any tier as a celebration cake without the topper, but include the simple circle decoration for the top, perhaps with the paisley and teardrop decoration inside.
- Simplify the paisley design used for the middle tier by omitting the piped dots.
- Simplify the paisley and teardrop decoration.

# small wonders

**Create these impressive jewelled miniature 'boxes' to make as gifts that suggest the mysterious East.**

Bake round cakes in 5cm (2in) multimini cake pans, or cut a larger cake into 5cm (2in) deep slices and then, using a 5cm (2in) circle cutter, cut the slices into rounds. Cut the hexagonal cakes using a 5cm (2in) side-to-side hexagonal cutter or template. Cover the cakes with sugarpaste as used for the main cake. Decorate each cake as you wish, using the cutters, pastes and inspiration from the main cake. You can make these cakes as simple or as involved as you like.

# falling leaf

Reminiscent of 1970s' design, this curled leaf creation would make an unusual wedding cake. It captures the end of summer with its golden and red hues, and is a mass of swirling patterns, creating a real sense of movement. The cake is formed from four stacked round cakes carved to shape. Templates for the basic curved decorative shapes that form the base of the design make creating this cake more straightforward than it might appear, and most of the details are made using cutters, embossers or texturing tools. Delightful leaf mini-cakes (below and on page 111) reflect the design.

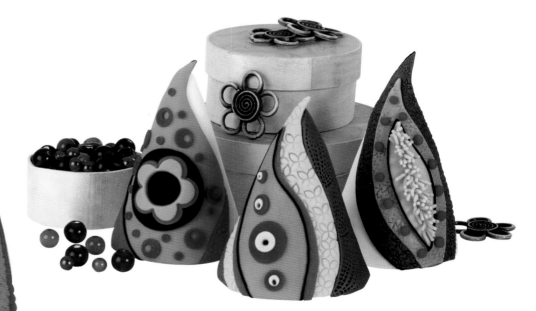

### Or make this cake for ...
• a retirement gift • anyone who loves the 1970s or retro fashion • a special birthday for an older person.

# you will need...

## materials

- 2.5kg (5lb 8oz) light-peach sugarpaste (rolled fondant)

- icing (confectioners') sugar (optional)

- white vegetable fat (shortening)

- cakes: 20cm (8in) round, 18cm (7in) round, 13cm (5in) round, 7.5cm (3in) round, baked in a food can to reach a height of 13cm (5in) (see pages 8–12)

- buttercream, or apricot glaze and marzipan (see pages 16–17)

- apricot jam (if using fruit cakes)

- clear spirit, such as gin or vodka

- modelling pastes: 75g (3oz) brown, 75g (3oz) yellow, 50g (2oz) gold, 50g (2oz) light orange, 50g (2oz) red, 100g (3½oz) dark orange, 50g (2oz) yellow-brown, 50g (2oz) ruby red, 50g (2oz) black, 50g (2oz) dark red, 50g (2oz) olive, 50g (2oz) light green, 50g (2oz) dark olive, 25g (1oz) light peach

- sugar glue (see page 14)

- paste colours for painting (optional): green, red, orange, yellow, brown

## equipment

- 5mm (³⁄₁₆in) spacers

- 28cm (11in) round cake drum (board)

- smoother

- palette knife

- poppy heads and Silicone Plastique, or poppy head moulds

- hardboard cake boards: 20cm (8in) round, 15cm (6in) round, 10cm (4in) round

- 7.5cm (3in) cake card, cut down to 6.5cm (2½in) round

- dowels

- cocktail stick (toothpick)

- scriber

- cutting wheel

- narrow spacers made from 1.5mm (¹⁄₁₆in) thick card

- sugar shaper with fine mesh, small and medium round discs

- Dresden tool

- ball tool

- piping tubes (tips) nos 18, 17, 16, 4, 3 (PME)

- mini embossers: curved zigzag (HP set 3, border designs), floral motif (HP set 2, side design), small flowers (HP set 1, small floral), grapes (HP set 11, vine and berry)

- craft knife

- pan scourer (new)

- fluting tool (JEM),

- quilting tool (PME)

- cutters: circle cutters: 6cm (2³⁄₈in) and 3.4cm (1¹¹⁄₃₂in) (FMM geometric set), 2.5cm (1in) and 2.1cm (²⁷⁄₃₂in) circles, five-petal flower from flat floral collection set 1 (LC), large blossom set (FMM)

- daisy centre stamps (JEM)

- half-ball moulds (PME)

- red and gold ribbons and non-toxic glue stick

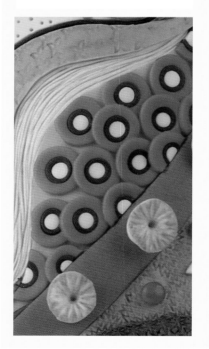

# preparation

## covering the board

Using 900g (2lb) of sugarpaste, cover the cake drum and trim the edges (see page 16). Place to one side to dry.

## making the poppy head mould

Select a range of poppy heads; you can use fresh or dried heads. Knead equal quantities of the two parts of the Silicone Plastique together. Roll balls of the mixture then flatten each. Take your poppy heads and press one into each flattened ball to make a selection of permanent poppy head moulds (**A**). Place to one side to dry.

## preparing the cake

1 If using Madeira, level the cakes and cut away the crusts. If using fruit cakes, invert them. Place each cake on the hardboard cake board or card that is slightly smaller than the cake. Dowel all except the top cake (see page 22). Spread a thin layer of buttercream or apricot jam over the top of each cake and stack the cakes.

2 Freeze the cake overnight if your freezer is large enough, if not chill the cake in the refrigerator – this helps with carving.

# stage one

## carving the cake

Mark the centre of the top cake with a cocktail stick, then take a large carving knife and cut down from the cocktail stick to the lower edge of the base cake to create a cone shape. Remove a little cake at a time and stand back from the cake occasionally to check that your cone is symmetrical. Place the cake on waxed paper.

## covering the cake

1 If using fruit cakes, cover with a layer of marzipan as described for the sugarpaste covering.

2 Using greaseproof paper make a template for the sugarpaste by holding one edge of the paper vertically against the side of the cake while wrapping the paper around the cake. Cut the paper vertically so that the two straight edges meet. Trim the excess from the base. You should have a circular segment slightly larger than quarter of a circle.

3 Cover the cake with a thin layer of buttercream (for sponge cakes) or clear spirit (for fruit).

4 Knead and roll out the sugarpaste between the 5mm (³/₁₆in) spacers to fit the template. Place the template on the paste and cut around it with a palette knife (if your paste is very soft you can add an extra 2.5cm (1in) margin to one side in case the paste stretches when you lift it).

5 Place the paste on your rolling pin with the curved outside edge of the segment hanging over one side and the tip/centre of the segment over the other. Position the curved edge at the base of the cake and carefully unroll the pin upwards to position the paste onto the cone. Using your hand and a smoother, position the cut sides of the paste so that they meet. Trim away the excess at the join with scissors and blend with a smoother. (If the join doesn't disappear, the leaf decoration can be positioned to cover any visible join.) Leave to dry.

# stage two

## scribing the cake

1 Using a pencil, trace the pattern of the leaf design on page 134 onto tracing or greaseproof paper. Cut the paper to the size of the template.

2 Place the template around the cake so that any visible join in the sugarpaste is covered. Secure the template in place with a few pins then scribe around the leaf (**B**) and add the design outlines by going over the pencil lines with a scriber. Check that you have scribed all of the design sections then remove all the pins and the template.

## the central vein

Roll the brown modelling paste into a long tapered sausage to fit the vein template. Flatten the paste slightly with a smoother. Cut out the central vein from the leaf template. Cut out the vein from the paste (**C**). Rub a finger over the cut edges to soften. Attach on to the cake using sugar glue.

## making the basic shapes

The basic shapes are made in sections as numbered on the sketch on page 109. Roll out each modelling paste between narrow spacers as detailed on the next page. Cut out the appropriate template and place on the paste. Cut around the template using a cutting wheel. Decorate as described. Attach to the cake with sugar glue.

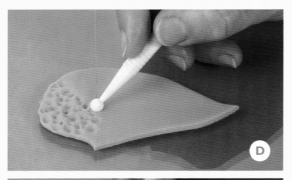

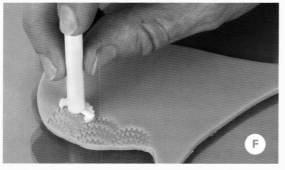

## section 1

Cut out and attach yellow paste. Soften some gold modelling paste by kneading in some white vegetable fat and boiled water until the consistency of chewing gum. Place in the sugar shaper with the fine mesh disc. Paint over the central area of the yellow section with sugar glue. Squeeze out short lengths of paste, removing them from the sugar shaper with the end of a Dresden tool, and attach them to the glued area.

## section 2

1 Cut out light orange paste. Texture by pressing the small end of the ball tool repeatedly into the paste (**D**). Attach to the cake.

2 Roll out red and dark orange paste. Cut six circles from red using the wide end of a piping tube. Remove an off-centre inner circle from each circle using a no. 18 tube. Attach on the orange section. Cut smaller dark-orange circles using the no. 16 tube and 'scatter' over the section.

## section 3

1 Cut out from yellow-brown paste (**E**). Texture by pressing the curved zigzag embosser repeatedly around the edge of the shape (**F**). Attach. Cut the two inner sections, as shown on the template, from two different shades of yellow paste and attach in position.

2 Roll a tapered sausage of ruby red paste to fit inside the smaller section and stick in place. Roll ten pea-sized balls of the same paste and place, equally spaced, within the yellow-brown border.

3 Use black paste in the sugar shaper with the small round disc. Paint a line of glue around the inner yellow shape and squeeze the paste over the glue (**G**). Cut to fit with a craft knife.

## section 4

1 Cut the red and orange pastes using the appropriate parts of the template. Attach the red shape. Press the pan scourer repeatedly into the surface of the orange shape for texture (**H**). Attach on top of the red shape so that it abuts the central vein. Attach a length of black paste from the sugar shaper around the outside edge of the orange paste.

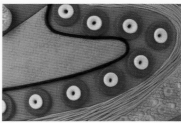

2 Cut out 12 dark-red circles, using the wide end of a piping tube and 12 yellow circles using a no. 18 tube. Place the yellow circles on top of the red and attach, equally spaced, within the red border. Cut the lower circles that abut the base with a craft knife to fit within the red border. Insert the pointed end of the fluting tool into the centre of each set of circles to reveal the red paste underneath.

## section 5

1 Cut out and attach dark red paste. Roll nine pea-sized balls from the same paste and attach in a random pattern to this section.

2 Use gold paste in the sugar shaper with the fine mesh disc. Paint around the edge of each red ball with sugar glue. Squeeze out short lengths of paste, and attach around the outside of each ball (**I**).

## section 6

1 Cut out and attach dark orange paste. Individually roll out black, red and yellow paste between narrow spacers. Using the wide end of a piping tube, cut circles from the red paste. Remove the circle centres using the no.18 tube.

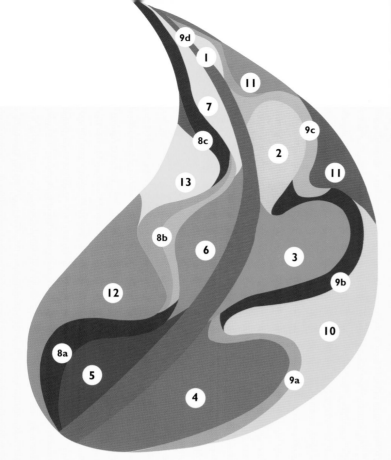

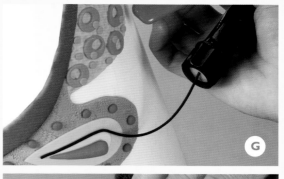

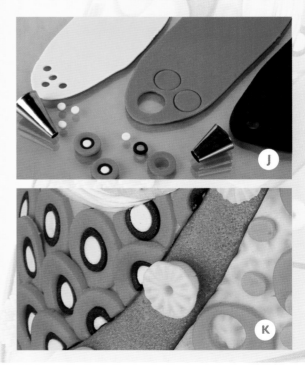

**2** Replace these circles with ones cut from the black paste. Blend the join between the two circles with your finger. Remove the centres from the black circles using a no. 16 tube, replacing them with yellow ones (**J**).

**3** Attach the circles to the cake in overlapping rows (**K**).

## section 7

Cut from yellow paste. Emboss with the mini floral motif embosser, and attach to the cake. Add orange and dark red shapes on top of the yellow so that they abut the central vein. Add black trim and small red, rolled balls to the yellow border.

## section 8

**1** Cut section 8(**a**) from the template from olive paste. Emboss all over with circles using the nos 16 and 3 piping tubes. Attach to the cake. With the no. 3 piping tube, remove circles of paste from within the larger circles to reveal the light-peach sugarpaste below.

**2** Cut the two 8(**b**) sections from the olive and light green pastes. Texture the olive with the small flower embosser. Attach the light green

section to the cake, and then texture it by running the wheel repeatedly along the length of the shape. Attach the olive section.

**3** Cut out and attach section 8(**c**) from dark olive. Texture using a quilting tool.

## section 9

Cut out and attach sections (**a**), (**b**), (**c**) and (**d**). Texture as for section 8 (see main picture).

## black trim

Place black paste and the small round disc in the sugar shaper. Squeeze out the paste around the outside edges of some of the green sections, referring to the pictures.

## section 10

**1** Cut out light-orange paste. Emboss with the mini grapes embosser. Attach. Using a 3.4cm (1¹¹⁄₃₂in) circle cutter, remove a circle of paste where the orange flower with the black surround will be placed and another circle to the right using the 2.5cm (1in) circle cutter. Remove randomly spaced circles using the no. 4 piping tube and add small orange

*A scriber is an excellent tool to help remove the cut circles.*

balls of paste in between the cut-out circles. Indent each ball with the head of a glass-headed pin.

2 Cut out a black 3.4cm (1¹¹/₃₂in) circle and a red and light-orange five-petal blossom. Place a smoother on top of the red blossom and press hard to flatten the paste and enlarge the flower. Place the red blossom and then the orange one on top of the black circle, and cut out the centre using the1.3cm (½in) wide daisy centre stamp (only remove the red and orange paste, not the black). Roll a ball of yellow paste and press it into the stamp, then attach inside the prepared flower (**L**). Attach.

3 Make the concentric circles using appropriate cutter sizes from red, orange and black paste. Make the red flower in the black circle and attach.

## section 11
Cut out and attach red and dark orange pastes.

## section 12
Cut out and attach dark orange paste. Cut a 6cm (2³/₈in) circle of black paste and make a larger version of the red and orange blossom made for section 10. Cut dark red circles using the no. 18 piping tube then remove smaller, off-centre circles from each one (**M**). Stick circles of both sizes to the area around the large flower.

## section 13
1 Cut out and attach yellow and red pastes. Add a red scroll to the yellow section using a sugar shaper with the small round disc.

2 Texture the yellow paste by pressing the end of a fluting tool into the paste around the scroll.

## poppy heads
Cut gold circles ranging in size from 5mm (³/₁₆in) to 2cm (¾in). Press each circle into an appropriate poppy-head mould and set aside (**N**). Roll balls

of gold modelling paste in a range of sizes from small pea to marble-sized. Press each into the smallest half-ball mould to make a range of half-balls. Attach these to the central vein of the leaf spacing them approximately 2cm (¾in) apart, placing the largest at the base of the leaf and the smallest at the tip. Add an appropriately sized embossed poppy head to each half-ball and then insert the fluting tool into the centre of each (**O**).

## leaf trim
Put some softened ruby modelling paste in the sugar shaper with the medium round disc. Paint sugar glue around the edges of the leaf. Squeeze out one length and place along one leaf edge. Cut to size with a craft knife. Repeat for the second side. Put some red paste in the sugar shaper and add another layer of trim (**P**). Add texture to this red trim by pressing the sharper end of the Dresden tool at regular intervals into the paste (**Q**).

## painting the cake
Dilute the suggested paste colours in clear spirit and paint over sections of the cake with a slightly darker colour to add depth to the textured sections and to make the cake even more vibrant. Leave to dry. Transfer the cake to the prepared board.

## the trim
Put some softened light-peach modelling paste in the sugar shaper with the medium round disc. Paint glue along the join between the cake and the board either side of the leaf design. Squeeze out a length of paste and position over the glue. Cut to fit with a craft knife and texture with the Dresden tool.

## finishing touches
Using a non-toxic glue stick attach the ribbons around the side of the cake drum.

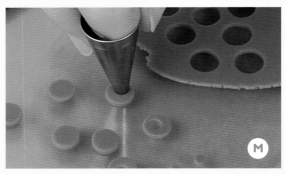

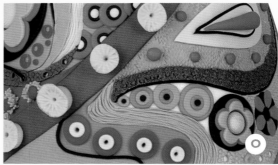

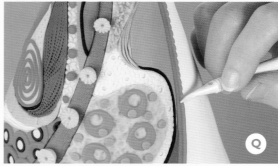

# love the look

- Use the various embossed and cut-out sections of the main cake as a band to go around a plain cake.
- Decorate a cake with some of the decorations used here, such as the overlapping concentric discs.
- Use the large flowers and poppy heads to decorate a cake based on a garden theme.

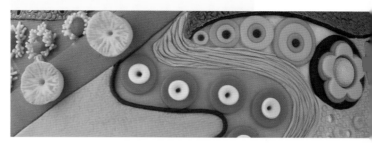

# simple shortcuts

- Choose your favourite embellishments from the leaf cake and add them to a shop-bought round cake.
- Use fewer patterns and simplify the cake.
- Use some of the ideas from the mini-cakes to make a boldly patterned smaller cake.
- Make a leaf shape to go on the top of a rectangular cake and decorate simply.
- Use the textures but fewer of the added shapes for a simple cake.

# small wonders

**Make a selection of leaf mini-cakes, each with its own unique design based on the main cake.**

Bake your cakes in 5cm (2in) multimini cake pans or alternatively cut a larger cake into 5cm (2in) deep slices and then, using a 5cm (2in) circle cutter, cut the slices into rounds. Carve the mini-cakes into cones as for the main cake. Cover the cakes with the light peach sugarpaste and decorate using a selection of the techniques and designs used for the main cake.

# sparkling fish

The Art Nouveau mosaics of Catalan architect Antoni Gaudi (1852–1926) were the inspiration for this unique irregular, stacked round cake with its silvery topper. It would make a spectacular piece for someone who loves mosaic art from the Mediterranean or who appreciates the unusual. Silvery fish swim across the smooth surfaces of the cakes, and the middle tier is covered with intricate mosaic waves – each tessera added by hand. Even the board is beautifully decorated, but the effect is not difficult to reproduce – just take your time. Dainty mosaic and fish mini-cakes (below and on page 117) make attractive gifts in the same theme.

### Or make this cake for ...
• someone who is a keen swimmer • the wedding of a couple who enjoy diving or other water sports • anyone who owns an aquarium or is fascinated by fish (the shape of the fish could be changed to match the recipient's favourite).

# you will need ...

## materials

- modelling paste: 50g (2oz) each of 12 different shades of blue from light to dark, 115g (4oz) white, 50g (2oz) grey

- white vegetable fat

- sugar glue (see page 14)

- sugarpaste (rolled fondant): 225g (8oz) mid blue, 2.25kg (4lb 15oz) white, 175g (6oz) pale blue

- cakes: 25.5cm (10in), 18cm (7in), 10cm (4in) round (see pages 8–12)

- buttercream, or apricot glaze and marzipan (see pages 16–17)

- clear spirit, such as gin or vodka (if using fruit cake)

- edible snowflake lustre dust

- ¼ quantity of royal icing

## equipment

- round cake drums (boards): 35.5cm (14in), 20cm (8in)

- small, sharp scissors

- glass-headed dressmakers' pins

- narrow spacers made from 1.5mm (¹⁄₁₆in) thick card

- set square

- craft knife

- paintbrushes

- palette knife

- piping tubes (tips) nos 18, 17, 16, 4 (PME)

- 1.5mm (⌡6/17g SWG/15g AWG) aluminium wire

- round-nosed pliers

- wire cutters

- round hardboard cake boards: 20cm (8in), 13cm (5in)

- waxed paper

- 7.5cm (3in) cake card (cut a larger one down to size)

- smoother

- small piece of clear flexible plastic, such as cut from a plastic bottle

- clear plastic, such as a plastic bag

- sugar shaper with small round disc

- scriber (optional)

- dowels

- posy pick

- oasis fix

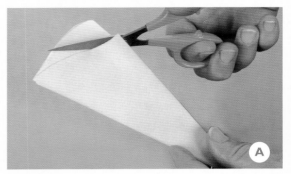

# preparation

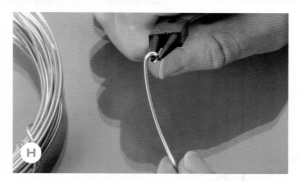

## preparing the board

1 Make a 35.5cm (14in) greaseproof paper circle by drawing around the 35.5cm (14in) cake drum. Fold the circle in half four times.

2 Draw a shallow S curve starting 2.8cm (1³/₃₂in) down from one top edge and finishing at the top of the other. Cut along this curve using scissors (**A**). Open out the template and place onto the drum; secure with pins. Draw around the curves of the template with a pencil (**B**).

3 Mark the centre of the board, then make a 20cm (8in) circle from greaseproof paper and fold in half twice to find the centre. Place the template centrally on the board by aligning the centres, and draw around the circle.

4 Turn the drum over and draw a 20cm (8in) circle on the base. Take the 20cm (8in) cake drum and stick it to the base of the board. (The mosaic tiles on the edge of the larger drum will be off the work surface, making them easier to create.)

## covering the board

1 Knead some dark blue modelling paste to warm it, adding a little white fat and/or boiled water to soften, if necessary.

2 Roll the paste out between narrow spacers. Using a set square and a craft knife, cut into 6mm (¼in) squares: cut the first line along one edge of the paste and then mark along the cut at 6mm (¼in) intervals. Position the set square along the line so that the point of the right angle corresponds to a mark. Cut through the paste at 90 degrees to the line. Reposition the set square, cut the next line and repeat to create strips. Mark 6mm (¼in) intervals along a strip. Place the set square along the strip so that the point of the right angle corresponds to a mark, then cut through the paste at 90 degrees to the line to create squares (**C**).

## adding the tiles

1 Paint sugar glue inside the wavy pencil line on the board. Lift and separate some of the mosaic tiles using a palette knife. Using a damp brush, place the tiles inside the pencil line on top of the glue, leaving a small gap between each tile (**D**). To achieve a close fit on the sharper curves remove a narrow tapered triangle from some of the squares when in place.

2 Roll out a lighter blue between the narrow spacers and cut into 4 x 10mm (¹/₈ x ³/₈in) rectangles. Paint sugar glue inside the previous line of tiles then position these rectangles end to end, but leaving a small gap, around the curve (certain tiles may need their shape adjusting slightly).

## adding circles

1 Cut out six circles using the wide end of one of the piping tubes and place them at the top of a curve on the next row, as shown. Cut 24 circles using the no. 4 tube and position two either side of each large circle. Cut circles using a no. 18 tube and stick so that they run parallel to the previous line of rectangles.

2 Continue adding rows of tiles, changing colour and shape with each row, to cover the board up to the inner 20cm (8in) circle.

## the sides of the board

For the sides of the board, cut 1.3cm (½in) squares in two different blues. Stick them, alternating the colours, to the sides of the board to lie flush with the top tiles (**E**).

## 'grouting' the tiles

1 Take 150g (5oz) of the mid-blue sugarpaste and place a little onto your workboard. Add boiled water and blend with a palette knife until a soft spreadable consistency.

2 Working in sections, spread the softened sugarpaste over some of the dried tiles so that the paste fills all the gaps between the tiles (**F**).

Remove as much excess paste as possible with the palette knife. Using folded, dampened kitchen towel, carefully remove all the remaining paste from the surface of the tiles (**G**).

## wire fish

1 Cut a 50cm (20in) length of aluminium wire. Clasp one end of the wire between round-nosed pliers and wrap the wire around one side of the pliers to create a circle in the wire (**H**).

2 Take the larger fish template on page 132 and place the wire circle over the fish's eye. Press down on the eye with the finger of one hand while bending the wire to shape following the lines of the template with your other hand. Reposition the finger that is pressing down on the wire as necessary (**I**). Once complete, bring the remaining length of the wire over to form a loop and then down below the fish. Make eight large fish and one smaller one.

# stage one

## carving and covering the cakes

1 Carve the cakes following the instructions on pages 19–20.

2 Stick the cakes onto their appropriate boards and card, and place on waxed paper. Cover the cakes following instructions on page 21. Leave to dry.

# stage two

## making the sugar fish

1 Place some clear plastic over the fish templates and trace onto the plastic using a pencil (the pencil will indent the surface to give a cutting line). Cut around the traced lines with a small pair of scissors.

2 Roll out some white modelling paste. Place the larger fish template onto the white paste and cut around it (**J**). Repeat to make eight larger fish and seven smaller ones.

3 Take a larger wire fish and position it over one of the cut-out paste fish. Press down firmly so the wire indents the paste (**K**). Repeat for the other fish, using the smaller wired fish for the smaller paste fishes. (**Note:** the two different sizes of fish swim in different directions.)

4 Soften some grey modelling paste by kneading in some white vegetable fat and boiled water. Put the paste in the sugar shaper with the small round disc. With a fine paintbrush paint a line of sugar glue into the indented areas of the fish.

5 Squeeze out some paste and place the end into the eye of the fish; continue squeezing and positioning the paste until the fish is complete (**L**). Trim to size and repeat for the remaining fish. Dust the fish with snowflake lustre dust (**M**).

6 Using sugar glue, attach the larger fish to the base tier and the smaller fish to the middle tier (see main picture).

## decorating the middle mosaic tier

1 Find the centre of the top of the middle tier then make a 7.5cm (3in) circle template. Place the template centrally on the cake and scribe around it with a scriber or pin.

2 Cut a range of mosaic tiles in different sizes, shapes and colours. Arrange the darker tiles along the backs of the lower fish then continue the curves down to the base of the cake. Add additional rows above and below the lower fish. Move on to the upper fish and repeat the process using lighter shades of tile.

3 Paint wave shapes over the top of the cake, using sugar glue. Attach rows of tiles over the glued curves (**N**). Fill in above and below the waves with more rows of tiles to cover the cake, apart from the scribed circle in the centre. Leave to dry.

# stage three

## completing the middle tier

Take most of the pale blue and mid-blue sugarpaste and soften each to a spreadable consistency. Working in sections, spread the mid-blue paste over the darker lower tiles and the light blue over the upper tiles, to fill the gaps between the tiles. Remove the excess. Leave to dry.

*If your finish isn't as smart as you would like, add a second layer of sugarpaste to disguise the irregularities.*

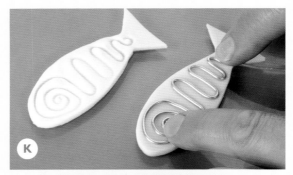

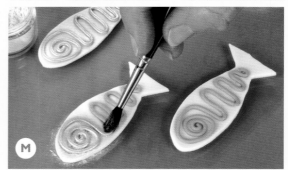

# stage four

## stacking the cakes

Remove the base tier from its waxed paper and place it centrally on the prepared cake drum. Dowel the base tier and the middle tier (see page 22). Attach the middle tier centrally on top of the base tier using royal icing to secure, and the top tier centrally to the middle tier so that the high side of one tier corresponds with the shallow side of another.

# stage five

## finishing detail

1 Cut 7mm (⁹/₃₂in) squares from dark and light blue modelling paste and glue the dark blue squares in a ring around the base of the lower tier and the light blue in a ring around the base of the top tier. Allow to dry.

2 Complete the mosaic rings by adding softened sugarpaste of the appropriate colour, as for the board and middle tier.

## arranging the topper

1 Insert a posy pick vertically into the centre of the cake with its surface fractionally below the surface of the sugarpaste.

2 Place a small amount of oasis fix into the posy pick to help secure the wires. Take a wire fish and gently create a wave in the wire. Cut to an appropriate length and insert into the posy pick. Repeat.

## love the look

- The cut-out fish could be used to decorate any simply iced cake; try using bright colours for the fish instead of white.
- Add a circle of mosaic to the top of an iced cake, and add a simple band of mosaic to go around the outside, if you like.
- Create the wire fish to decorate a simply iced blue cake.
- Change the colours to create a bright tropical coral reef.

## simple shortcuts

- Cover the board with plain dark blue sugarpaste instead of using the mosaic trim.
- Make a two-tiered cake using the upper two tiers and add the fish topper.
- Use the lower tiers and cover the whole of the top with mosaic. Omit the fish.
- Make it a stacked cake using round cakes rather than an angled cake.

## small wonders

**For a hint of sunlit pools, make these stylish little mini-cakes decorated with mosaic or wired fish.**

Bake your cakes in 5cm (2in) multimini cake pans or cut a larger cake into 5cm (2in) deep slices, and then use a 5cm (2in) circle cutter to cut the slices into rounds. Cover the cakes with the sugarpaste used for the main cake. Decorate the cakes with a selection of the mosaic patterns and small sugar and wire fish as used for the main cake

# luxurious orchid wedding

One of the most exquisite flowers, the moth orchid, is the focal point of this unique creative wedding cake, whose colours can be matched to the fabric of the bride's or bridesmaids' outfit. The design uses a combination of cake shapes, topped by a ball, with two of the tiers made from petal-shaped cakes. The whole arrangement extends elegantly upwards using a stylish separator and a wired-bead fountain. Make the delicate orchids using special cutters and flower paste; the remaining decorations are simple to achieve although no less eye-catching.

Perfectly created mini-cakes, see below and page 125, make ideal individual gift cakes for the guests or bridal party.

### Or make this cake for …
• Mother's Day – simply make the top orchid ball cake as an exquisite gift • bonfire night – cover a simple round cake and add brightly coloured flames • a wedding anniversary or an engagement • a birthday – any tier or element of this cake can be adapted for a birthday cake, with wide appeal from a teenage girl's birthday to any adult who loves flowers.

119

# you will need ...

## materials

- sugarpaste (rolled fondant): 1.8kg (4lb) pink with a touch of blue (for the board), 1kg (2¼lb) pale pink, 3kg (6lb 10oz) pink, 300g (11oz) white with a touch of pink

- icing (confectioners') sugar (optional)

- white vegetable fat (shortening)

- cakes: 35.5cm (14in) petal, 25.5cm (10in) round, 18cm (7in) petal, 10cm (4in) ball (see pages 8–12)

- buttercream or apricot glaze and marzipan (see pages 16–17)

- paste colours: ruby/rose, burgundy, yellow (either sunflower (SK) or egg yellow (SF), blue

- gum tragacanth

- clear spirit, such as gin or vodka

- Superwhite dust colour

- sugar glue (see page 14)

- 1 quantity of royal icing

- 200g (7oz) white flower paste (petal/gum paste)

- edible dust colours: plum, deep yellow, snowflake (SK)

## for the beaded topper

- a selection of beads to match the cake; Lindy used:
  - 8mm (⁵⁄₁₆in) cerise miracle beads
  - 8mm (⁵⁄₁₆in) pink crackle beads
  - 6mm (¼in) shocking pink glass pearls
  - 6mm (¼in) pink glass pearls
  - ivory freshwater pearls
  - gold and pink silver-lined rocailles

- 24 gauge silver floristry wire

- strong acrylic glue

- posy pick

- oasis fix

## equipment

- 5mm (³⁄₁₆in) spacers

- cake drums (boards): 46cm (18in) round, 23cm (9in) round, 30cm (12in) round

- smoother

- palette knife

- silver trumpet separator (LC)

- glass-headed dressmakers' pin

- waxed paper

- 25.5cm (10in) round hardboard cake board

- dowels

- 7.5cm (3in) round cake card

- small, sharp scissors

- selection of brushes including a stippling, a dusting brush and paintbrushes

- sugar shaper with small round and medium round discs

- craft knife

- piping tubes: nos 1 and 2

- disposable piping bags

- 13cm (5in) round cake card

- scriber

- tracing paper

- Dresden tool

- life-size moth orchid cutter set (LC)

- clear plastic, such as a plastic bag

- foam pad

- ball tool

- moth orchid veiner (GI–M75235)

- dimpled foam

- 1 pale pink and 1 mid pink ribbon, and non-toxic glue stick

- non-slip matting

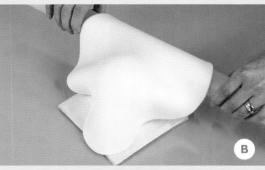

**A**

**B**

**C**

**D**

**E**

# preparation

## covering the boards

**1** Roll out the darkest pink sugarpaste between 5mm (³/₁₆in) spacers using icing sugar or white vegetable fat to prevent sticking. Lift up the paste and place it over the 46cm (18in) round cake drum. Use a smoother to smooth the paste level. Trim the edges flush with the sides of the board using a palette knife.

**2** To mark the separator position on the base of the 23cm (9in) round cake drum, make two paper circles, one by drawing around the drum and one by drawing around the separator's base plate. Fold the circles in half and half again to find their centres. Place the 23cm (9in) circle on the underside of the drum and mark the drum's centre with a pin.

Remove the paper circle and replace with the smaller one. Draw around the edge to mark its position (**A**). Remove and replace with the separator. Draw around its base with a pencil. Keep the paper templates.

**3** Cover the 23cm (9in) drum using some of the pale pink sugarpaste. Leave to dry.

## stage one

### covering the cakes

**1** **Large petal cake** Place the cake on top of the 30cm (12in) cake drum, then stand it on waxed paper. Cover with buttercream or apricot glaze and marzipan. Roll out 2kg (4½lb) of the pink sugarpaste between 5mm (³/₁₆in) spacers and use to cover the cake. Ease the paste into shape, especially around the petals. Smooth the top and sides of the cake with a smoother and your palm. Trim the base, using a smoother to create a line, and a palette knife.

**2** **Round cake** Place the cake onto the 25.5cm (10in) round hardboard and then place it on waxed paper. Cover the cake with buttercream or apricot glaze and marzipan then pink sugarpaste.

**3** **Small petal cake** Place the cake centrally on waxed paper. Insert three dowels into the central area of the cake (see page 22), and place the 7.5cm (3in) card on top. Cover the cake with buttercream or apricot glaze and marzipan then with pale pink sugarpaste.

**4** **Ball cake** Place the cake on waxed paper and cover with buttercream or apricot glaze and marzipan. Roll out the white-with-a-touch-of-pink sugarpaste and place over the ball cake (**B**). Ease around the base of the cake and pull up the excess to form two pleats. Cut the

pleats away with scissors (**C**) and smooth the joins closed with your hand. Trim the excess paste away from the base of the cake. Using a smoother and your hand, smooth the surface of the cake with vertical strokes (**D**). Leave to dry.

*It is worth spending time doing this; the paste will not dry out if you continually work it.*

### making modelling paste

Using the sugarpaste trimmings and the paste colours, create 115g (4oz) each of deep pink, mid pink, pale pink, burgundy and a warm yellow. Add 2.5ml (½ tsp) gum tragacanth to each to make modelling paste. Leave for 2 hours or overnight (ideally) to mature.

### painting the boards

**1** **Largest board** Dilute the rose paste colour in clear spirit and mix in the Superwhite dust to create pink paint. Adjust the colour by adding a touch of blue. Try out the mixed paint on some of the sugarpaste trimmings and adjust as necessary, especially if you wish to match the colour with a fabric sample (**E**).

With a stippling brush stipple the edge of the covered board. Paint the vertical sugarpaste edge to the board. Reserve the remaining paint for the large petal cake.

**2** **Smaller board** Mix the Superwhite dust colour with clear spirit to make white paint, then add enough ruby/rose paste colour to make it a little darker than the sugarpaste of the board.

**3** Stipple the edge of the covered board and then paint the vertical sugarpaste edge. Reserve the remaining paint for the small petal cake. Allow to dry.

# stage two

## painting the cakes

1 **Large petal cake** Using the reserved paint from the largest board, stipple into the six petal recesses in a roughly triangular pattern, to create a shadow effect.

2 Mix up some paint a fraction darker than the sugarpaste of the large petal cake, using paste colours, Superwhite dust and clear spirit. Stipple over the sides of the cake with a dry brush for a mottled effect. Blend the paint with the darker shade already applied. Bring the colour up over the top of the cake and paint the area that will be visible (**F**).

3 **Round cake** Using a dry brush, stipple partially up the sides of the cake with the paint mixed for the large petal cake, with the colour strongest at the base and fading as it moves up the sides.

4 **Small petal cake** Using the reserved paint from the smaller board and a fairly dry brush, paint the lower sides of the cake, ensuring that the colour is strongest at the base and fades as it goes up.

5 **The ball cake** Mix up paint to match the sugarpaste of the small petal cake, then stipple around the lower third of the ball. Allow to dry.

*The depth of colour will depend on how much paint you have on your brush so it is a good idea to experiment on some spare sugarpaste first.*

# stage three

## the small petal cake

1 Transfer the cake to the 23cm (9in) prepared drum. Soften some pale pink modelling paste by kneading in some white vegetable fat and partially dunking the paste into boiled water before kneading again. Place into the sugar shaper with the small round disc and squeeze out a length. Place the length around the base of the cake, cut to size and secure with sugar glue.

2 For the flame shapes, knead half of each of the modelling pastes, then break into small pieces and scatter over your work surface to mix up the colours (**G**). Gather them into a ball and briefly knead together. Cut across the ball to reveal the marbled pattern inside. Place the two half-balls together and then roll out the paste using white vegetable fat to prevent sticking (**H**). The direction you roll the paste will affect the marbled pattern, so try

altering the rolling direction as the pattern develops.

3 Cut freehand flame shapes with a craft knife (**I**) so that the marbled lines go along the length of the flame. Attach to the cake using sugar glue.

4 To pipe the dots, colour some royal icing a very deep pink and some mid pink. Check the consistency of the icing by adding more sugar or boiled water, if necessary, to make round dots and not pointed cones.

5 Fit a no. 2 tube to a piping bag, and add a line of each coloured icing into the bag (**J**). Carefully fold over the bag and squeeze both colours into the tube at the same time. Pipe dots around the lower half of the cake in between the flames (**K**); vary the size of the dots by squeezing the tube more (for larger dots) or less (for smaller dots). Repeat using two lighter pink shades of royal icing, and piping further up the cake (**L**).

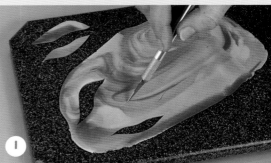

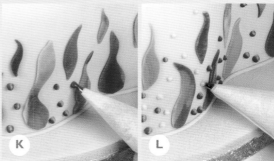

## decorating the round cake

1. Find the centre of the cake using your paper templates and mark the position of the separator by scribing around the smaller template. Position the 13cm (5in) cake card within the circle and paint a line of sugar glue onto the cake around the card.

2. Using the sugar shaper and the medium round disc, squeeze out a length of pale pink paste to go around the card. Place in position and cut to fit. Remove the card.

3. Create some marbled paste and cut large flame shapes using the cake card to help shape the blunt end of the flame (**M**). Attach the flames to the cake with sugar glue so that they radiate from the central circle (**N**). Add smaller flames to the sides of the cake. Pipe dots as before.

## decorating the large petal cake

1. Transfer the cake to the prepared board. Trace the swirl patterns on page 132 onto tracing paper. Fold the paper vertically between the two swirls. Place the tracing with the fold in the recess of a petal (**O**). Transfer the design onto the cake using a pencil. Repeat for each recess.

2. Paint a line of sugar glue around the base of the cake. Using mid-pink modelling paste and the sugar shaper with medium round disc, squeeze out a length of paste and place it on the glue. Cut it to size. Use the sharp end of a Dresden tool and indent a textured pattern into the paste.

3. Using a fine paintbrush paint over the traced scrolls with sugar glue. Using softened burgundy modelling paste and the sugar shaper with the small round disc, squeeze out a length of paste and place it over a glued scroll; cut to size. Repeat.

4. Add royal icing dots between the scrolls for decoration.

*Don't overdo the glue as it may remove the paint.*

## the beaded topper

1. Select beads to match the cake. Dip the end of a 24 gauge wire into acrylic glue, and place a bead on top of the glue. Leave horizontally to dry. To create wires with several beads, use a cocktail stick (toothpick) to place a dot of glue on the wire for the bead furthest from the end. Thread the bead onto the wire so that it rests on the glue dot. Continue until the desired effect is created. Make different combinations of beaded wires; you will need three to six of each of your chosen types, plus one for the centre (**P**).

2. Insert the posy pick vertically into the centre of the ball cake (**Q**) so that its top lies flush with the top of the sugarpaste covering the cake.

## the moth orchids

1 Smear white vegetable fat over your work board to prevent sticking. Roll out some white flower paste very thinly. Using the moth orchid cutters, cut one dorsal (central) sepal, two lateral (lower) sepals and two petals (the largest cutter). Tint some flower paste pink and cut out one lip for each flower. Cover with clear plastic to prevent them from drying out.

2 Place a sepal onto the foam pad. Using the ball tool, stroke around the edges of the paste by pressing the tool half on the paste and half on the pad to soften the cut edge. Place the sepal in the double-sided moth orchid veiner. Press down hard on the top of the veiner then release. Remove the paste (**R**). Place the sepal onto dimpled foam and leave to dry partially. Repeat for the remaining sepals and petals.

3 Arrange the sepals and petals in groups as shown (**S**). Attach them onto the large petal cake using royal icing so that the top and lateral sepals lie under the larger side petals.

4 For the lip, soften the edges of the paste with a ball tool then cup the two side lobes by gently circling a ball tool in their centres. Roll three tiny sausages of paste, add two for the callus and one onto the tip of the lip for the lip tendril (**T**). Using a dry dusting brush, dip the tip of the brush into a pot of plum dust, tap off the excess and dust the edges of the lip. Add deep yellow dust to the centre.

5 Dilute some burgundy paste colour in clear spirit and add markings using a fine paintbrush. Place the lips onto the cupped area of dimpled foam and allow to dry sufficiently so that the cupped shape is maintained when handled.

6 Place a dot of royal icing in the centre of each flower on the cake and attach the lips in place. Roll six small balls of white flower paste and stick onto the central point of the flower to represent a pearl.

*Try to arrange the flowers while there is still some flexibility in the flower paste; once they are dry they are very brittle.*

## stacking the cakes

Dowel the large petal cake and the round cake. Using royal icing, attach the round cake on top of the large petal cake. Attach the separator to the round cake, and the ball cake to the small petal cake. Allow the icing to dry.

## decorating the top tier – ball cake

1 Using softened pale pink modelling paste and the sugar shaper and medium round disc, add trim to the base of the ball cake. Texture the trim with a Dresden tool.

2 Colour some flower paste pink and create three moth orchid flowers with pink petals and sepal, and a white throat. Attach so they are evenly spaced around the ball and line up with the petals of the cake below

## arranging the cake topper

1 Place a little oasis fix into the posy pick. Take a beaded wired and gently curve the wire by wrapping it around a cylinder such as a can or roll of tape (**U**). Cut the wire as appropriate and insert it into the posy pick.

2 Create the shape of the topper by arranging some curved wires of the same length around the base of the fountain. Using a few straight wired beads, define the height. It helps to stand back occasionally while arranging the wires to get an overall impression of the shape.

3 Fill in the spaces with the remaining beads, making sure that they are evenly spaced.

## finishing touches

Add pink trim to the base of the second tier using the sugar shaper and small round disc. Using a non-toxic glue stick attach the ribbons around the sides of the two cake drums.

## assembling the cake

Place the non-slip matting on the top plate of the separator. Position the top tier so that the separator lines up with the drawn circle on the underside of the cake drum, and the petals of the top cake line up with those on the base.

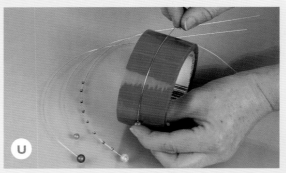

# love the look...

• Use the beautiful moth orchids to add a feminine touch to any birthday cake.
• Simple sugar piping swirls add a quick and easy stylish touch – use a bright colour to complement your cake.

# simple shortcuts

• For a smaller but no less dramatic cake in half the time, use just the ball cake and the petal cake (as shown left)
• Make either a petal or round flame cake with a simple icing flower decoration in its centre.
• Continue the delicate piped balls over the ball cake instead of adding the moth orchids for a simple but striking version.

# small wonders

**For a stylish floral finish, make mini versions of the same moth orchid flowers as for the main cake.**

Cut a cake into 3cm (1⅛in) deep slices. Using either a 6.5cm (2½in) wide six-petal flower cutter or the template on page 132, cut out as many flower cakes as required. Cover each cake with pink sugarpaste and decorate with a small moth orchid flower, using the technique described opposite, with smaller cutters. Neaten the base of each cake by adding a dark pink trim, using the sugar shaper and small round disc.

125

# cosmic christmas ball

Celebrate Christmas in style with this stunning departure from the ordinary. A ball cake covered with ivory sugarpaste sits on a golden painted board and is surrounded by swirls of wires and beads that appear to move before your eyes. Twinkling gold and ivory stars project from the ball adding to the overall appearance of movement and light. There are no complicated modelling techniques here, and the free form of the wires makes this amazing effect straightforward to reproduce. For extra sparkle make the accompanying mini-cakes (below and on page 131) as Christmas gifts.

## Or make this cake for …
• a golden wedding anniversary • a cake for a small wedding – the colours could match the bridesmaid's dresses if you like • an eighteenth or twenty-first birthday.

# you will need ...

## materials

- sugarpaste (rolled fondant): 1.6kg (3½lb) ivory
- icing (confectioners') sugar (optional)
- white vegetable fat (shortening)
- paste colours: golden brown (Spectral: autumn leaf), cream
- clear spirit, such as gin or vodka
- pastillage: 25g (1oz) ivory, 25g (1oz) gold
- large ball cake (see pages 8–12)
- buttercream, or apricot glaze and marzipan (see pages 16–17)
- edible lustre dust: brilliant gold
- confectioners' glaze
- ¼ quantity of royal icing

## equipment

- 5mm (³/₁₆in) spacers
- 25.5cm (10in) round cake drum (board)
- smoother
- palette knife
- paintbrushes
- cocktail stick (toothpick)
- narrow spacers made from 1.5mm (¹/₁₆in) thick card
- elegant star cutters (LC)
- foam pad
- waxed paper
- small, sharp scissors
- antique-gold or copper ribbon and non-toxic glue stick
- crystal stars (CB C-01 and B-04)

## for the beaded decoration

- posy pick
- dowel
- wires: 2mm (14g SWG/12g AWG) aluminium wire, 0.6mm (23g SWG/22g AWG) gold-plated jewellery wire, lilac metallic reel wire, lavender bullion wire
- wire cutters
- an assortment of beads, crystals and pearls; Lindy used:

  pearls: 12mm (¹⁵/₃₂in) gold and silver, 6mm (¼in) silver and ivory, 4mm (¹/₈in) ivory

Japanese rocailles – lavender and gold

lilac moon star lamp beads

6mm (¼in) burnt orange miracle beads

Swarovski crystals: crystal pearls in gold and copper; crystal hearts in topaz, light amethyst and crystal

5mm (³/₁₆in) square faceted crystals

- gold crimps
- flat-nosed pliers
- oasis fix

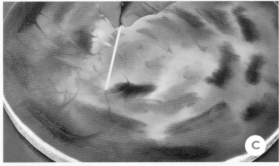

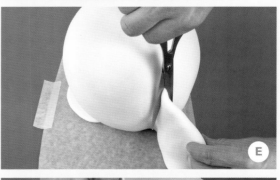

# preparation

### covering the board

Knead 700g (1½lb) of ivory sugarpaste to warm it and then roll the paste out between 5mm (³⁄₁₆in) spacers, using icing sugar or white vegetable fat to prevent sticking. Lift up the paste, using a rolling pin for support, and place it over the board. Take a smoother and, using a circular motion, smooth the paste to give a level surface. Using a palette knife, trim the edges flush with the sides of the board, taking care to keep the cut vertical. Place to one side to dry.

### colouring the board (flood painting)

1 Separately slightly dilute the golden brown and cream paste colours with clear spirit. Take a paintbrush and roughly paint each colour in circular bands over the board leaving some areas white (**A**).

2 Carefully pour clear spirit or cooled boiled water over the partially painted surface (**B**). Then use a paintbrush to encourage the liquid to cover the board entirely. (You may wish to try this effect on a spare piece of sugarpaste first, as it does appear to be rather drastic!) The liquid will melt the surface of the paste so that the colours merge – be patient because this takes a while.

3 Once the sugarpaste has turned syrupy (this will take between 30 minutes and 1 hour, or perhaps even longer, depending on the temperature and humidity you are working in), take a cocktail stick or thin paintbrush and draw figures of eight through the sugar syrup to transfer colour from one area of the board to another (**C**). Make the figures of eight radiate out from the centre of the board and overlap them to create a swirling pattern. Leave the board undisturbed on a level surface to dry thoroughly.

### making the pastillage stars

Roll out ivory pastillage between the narrow spacers and cut out a selection of stars (**D**). Repeat using the gold pastillage. Place the stars on a foam pad and leave to dry thoroughly.

*An airing cupboard is an ideal place to dry pastillage.*

# stage one

### covering the cake

1 Place the cake on waxed paper. If using a fruit cake cover with apricot glaze and marzipan, following the instructions for sugarpaste below.

2 To help the sugarpaste stick to the cake, cover with a thin layer of buttercream (for a sponge cake) or paint over the marzipan with clear spirit (for a fruit cake).

3 Roll out the ivory sugarpaste into a circle between the 5mm (³⁄₁₆in) spacers and place over the cake. Ease the paste around the base of the cake and pull up the excess to form two pleats. Cut the pleats away with scissors (**E**) and smooth the joins closed; they should disappear quite readily with the heat of your hand. Trim the excess paste away from the base of the cake. Next, using a smoother followed by your hand, smooth the surface of the cake with vertical strokes (**F**). Set the cake aside to dry.

*It is worth spending time doing this – the paste will not dry out if you continually work it.*

# stage two

### creating the beaded decoration

1 Take a posy pick and insert it into the cake 5cm (2in) below the top of the cake (**G**).

2 Place the dowel into the posy pick, then take the aluminium wire and wrap the end around the dowel near to the mouth of the posy pick to secure it. Next, make a large loop in the wire and then wrap the wire around the dowel again to secure the loop (**H**). Continue until you have made five loops. Secure the last loop and cut the wire.

**Note: the wire and bead decoration should not touch the cake and should be removed from the cake before it is carved.**

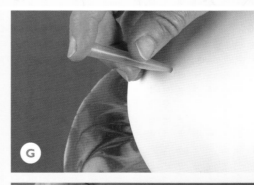

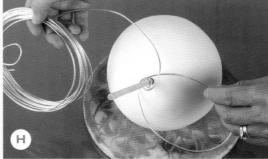

**3** Shape each loop into more of an organic form, bending each one back over the shape of the cake without touching the icing (**I**).

## threading the beads

**1** Next, cut a 1.5m (5ft) length of gold jewellery wire. Using all your selected beads except the crystal hearts, alternately thread on a crimp, a bead, or an arrangement of three beads followed by two crimps – will need a total of around 60–100 beads on the wire, depending on which you choose to use.

**2** Position a crimp 5cm (2in) from one end of the wire and squeeze it onto the wire using pliers. Move the nearest bead(s) and the next crimp up to the first crimp, and squeeze the second crimp in place so that the bead cannot move along the wire. Leave a gap of 6–12cm (2⅜–4¾in) and repeat (**J**) until you have secured all the beads.

## adding the beaded wire

**1** Wrap one end of the gold wire around the dowel above the aluminium wire to secure it, as you did for the aluminium wire. Then make loops as before, although not quite as large, until you have a total of five. Secure the last loop and cut the wire. Shape each loop to give the wires a pleasing effect.

**2** Take the lilac metallic reel wire, attach the end to the dowel by forming a tight loop then form five additional loops as before, but as you do so try not to straighten out the wire too much – allow the wire to slip off the end of the reel rather than unwinding it. Then do the same using the lavender bullion wire.

*The secret of an even twist is releasing the wire with even pressure*

## fixing the decoration in place

**1** To make a wire 'peg', take a 30cm (12in) length of aluminium wire and bend one end to form a small series of loops leaving the other end straight (**K**).

Cut a few lengths of metallic reel wire. Carefully remove the dowel plus wires from the cake. Then carefully slide the dowel out, holding the wires stable at the same time. Thread the cut metallic wire lengths through the coiled wires and around the outside, and then twist the ends tightly together to secure all the wires in place.

**2** Place a small sausage of oasis fix inside the posy pick. Place the straight length of aluminium wire from the peg through the centre of the secured coils and then into the posy pick, thus securing the wires to the cake (**L**).

## adding crystal hearts

**1** Take the crystal hearts and the lavender bullion wire. Cut the bullion wire into 5cm (2in) lengths. Thread a crystal heart onto a cut wire and place in the centre of the wire, then, using your thumb and index finger of one hand, hold the crystal in place while you bring the wires together with your thumb and index finger of the other hand so that the crystal is locked into position. Twist the crystal repeatedly while slowly allowing the wire in your other hand to slide through your fingers to obtain an even twist (**M**). Repeat for the remaining crystal hearts.

**2** Decide where the crystals are to be added to the lilac metallic and lavender bullion wire and twist them into position so that they are secure but hang down from the wire they have been attached to (**N** and **O**).

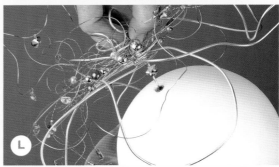

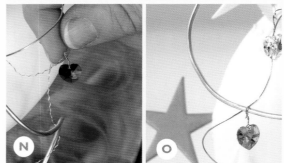

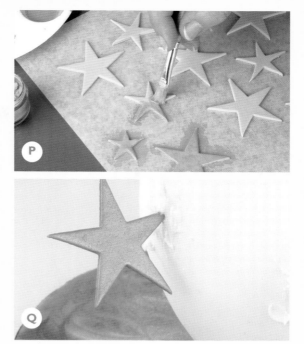

## adding the stars

1 Place the dried gold pastillage stars onto waxed paper. Mix the gold lustre dust with confectioners' glaze to create paint, then, using a paintbrush, paint around the sides and over the top of each star (**P**). Allow the glaze to dry (this should take only a few minutes), then turn over the stars and paint the other face.

2 Colour the royal icing so that it matches the sugarpaste of the ball. Place some onto the back of a palette knife and stipple a small section of the ball with the icing. Insert an ivory or gold star through the royal icing into the cake (once the icing is dry it will hold the star securely in place) (**Q**). Repeat until you are happy with the number of stars.

## finishing touches

Using a non-toxic glue stick, attach the ribbon around the sides of the board. Finally, attach the crystal stars randomly on top of the ribbon using non-toxic glue.

## love the look

- Use a few giant stars to decorate the top of a plain cake, or lots of little ones all over.
- Add the beaded ornament to any plain, iced round cake (you could simplify the beading if you like).
- The pendant crystal hearts would make a delicate touch for any simple wired cake decoration.

## simple shortcuts

- Use either either aluminium wire or 0.6mm (23g SWG/22g AWG) jewellery wire to make a simplified version of the ornament.
- Make a simple fountain of wires topped with beads (based on the topper on page 123).
- Use a simplified version of the beaded decoration to go on a plain round cake.

## small wonders

**Decorate mini-cakes with stars or a tiny version of the beaded ornament to create fun miniature festive gifts.**

Bake your cakes in 5cm (2in) multimini cake pans or cut a larger cake into 5cm (2in) deep slices and then use a 5cm (2in) circle cutter to cut the slices into rounds. Cover the cakes with the ivory coloured sugarpaste used for the main cake. Decorate with a selection of the smaller stars, a miniature version of the beaded wire decoration or add a mini beaded garland using the beads used for the main cake.

# Templates

The templates on the following pages are shown at 100% size, unless indicated.
Templates shown at 50% size should be enlarged on a photocopier at 200%.

fish (large)

fish (small)

Sparkling Fish (page 112)

Luxurious Orchid Wedding
template for mini-cake
(page 118)

Greek Inspirations (page 78)
scribing template for scrolls

Luxurious Orchid Wedding
(page 118) swirl template

Connoisseur's Delight (page 64)
scribing template
(enlarge by 200%)

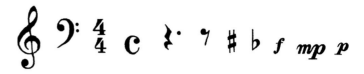

musical symbols

music

Perfect Harmony (page 50)
(enlarge by 200%)

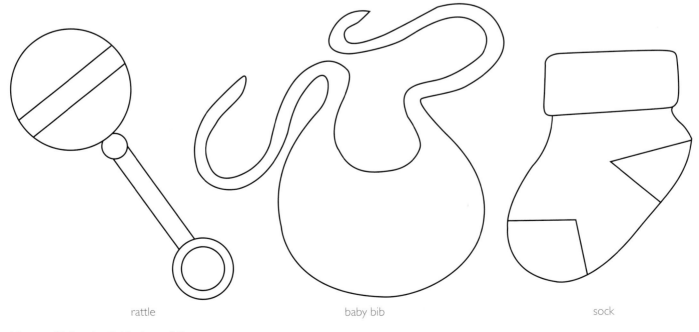

rattle

baby bib

sock

Nursery Christening Bricks (page 84)

Eastern Ornament (page 96)
wire template

lily (small)

lily template for
mini-cakes

lily (large)

Art Nouveau Lilies (page 42)

Falling Leaf (page 104)
scribing template sketch of sections
(enlarge by 200%)

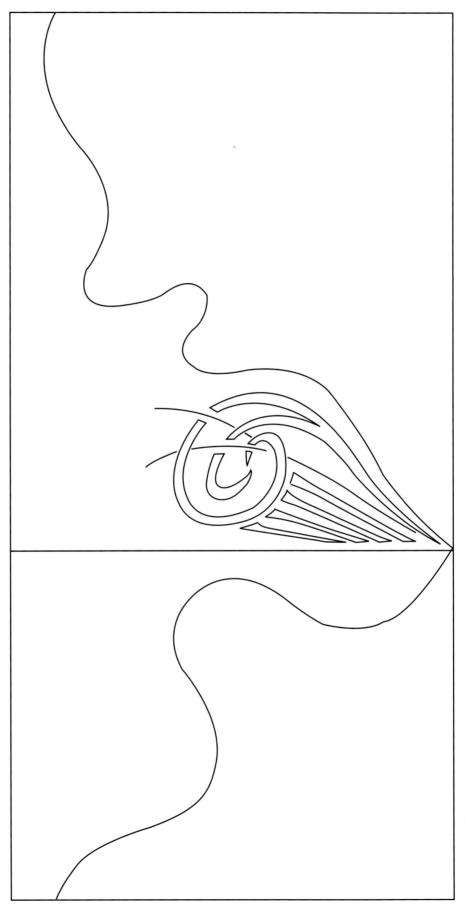

Art Nouveau Lilies (page 42)
scribing template
(enlarge by 200%)

# acknowledgments

I would like to thank: M&B for supplying me with their superb range of sugarpaste, as always, it has been a delight to use and has saved me hours of colouring time; Marion from Patchwork Cutters for being so generous with her wonderful cutters – they are a pleasure to use; Andy, my PA/manager/cake coordinator, for all her hard work keeping Lindy's Cakes Ltd running smoothly while I created this book and for providing most of the sponge cakes for photography – Andy you now have cakes in print! Also, thanks to my readers, from every corner of the globe, who have contacted me with their kind comments and requests.

A special thank you also goes to my family for all their input, opinions and encouragement.

## suppliers

### UK

**Alan Silverwood Ltd (AS)**
Ledsam House
Ledsam Street
Birmingham B16 8DN
tel: +44(0)121 454 3571
email: sales@alan-silverwood.co.uk
www.alansilverwood.co.uk

*Manufacturer of multisized cake pan, multimini cake pans and spherical moulds/ball tins (pans)*

**Ceefor Cakes**
PO Box 443
Leighton Buzzard
Bedfordshire LU7 1AJ
tel: +44(0)1525 375237
email: ceefor.cakes@virgin.net
www.ceeforcakes.co.uk

*Supplier of strong cake boxes – most sizes available*

**FMM Sugarcraft (FMM)**
Unit 5
Kings Park Industrial Estate
Primrose Hill
Kings Langley
tel: +44 (0)1923 268699
email: clements@f-m-m.demon.co.uk
www.fmmsugarcraft.com

*Manufacturer of cutters*

**Holly Products (HP)**
Primrose Cottage
Church Walk
Norton in Hales
Shropshire TF9 4QX
www.hollyproducts.co.uk

*Manufacturer and supplier of embossing sticks and moulds*

**Lindy's Cakes Ltd (LC)**
17 Grenville Avenue
Wendover
Bucks HP22 6AG
tel: +44(0)1296 623906
email: mailorder@lindyscakes.co.uk
www.lindyscakes.co.uk

*Manufacturer of cutters and cake separators plus mail-order equipment and cake jewellery supplies as used in Lindy's books*

**M&B Specialised Confectioners Ltd**
3a Millmead Estate
Mill Mead Road
London N17 9ND
tel: +44(0)20 8801 7948
email: info@mbsc.co.uk
www.mbsc.co.uk

*Manufacturer and supplier of sugarpaste*

**Patchwork Cutters (PC)**
3 Raines Close
Greasby, Wirral
CH49 2QB
tel: +44(0)151 6785053
email: info@patchworkcutters.com
www.patchworkcutters.com

*Manufacturer and supplier of cutters and embossers*

### US

**Global Sugar Art**
7 Plattsburgh Plaza
Plattsburgh, NY 12901
tel: 518-561-3039
email: info@globalsugarart.com
www.globalsugarart.com

**Cake Craft Shoppe**
3530 Highway 6
Sugar Land, Texas 77478
tel: 281-491-3920
email: info@cakecraftshoppe.com
www.cakecraftshoppe.com

**Country Kitchen**
4621 Speedway Drive
Fort Wayne
Indiana 46825
tel: +1 800 497 3927 or 219482 4835
www.countrykitchensa.com

### Australia

**Cake Deco**
Shop 7, Port Phillip Arcade
232 Flinders Street
Melbourne, Victoria
tel: (03) 9654 5335
www.cakedeco.com.au

*Mail-order cake supplier*

**Iced Affair**
53 Church Street
Camperdown, NSW 2050
tel: (02) 9519 3679
www.icedaffair.com.au

*Mail-order supplier*

**Abbreviations used in the book:**

| | |
|---|---|
| AS | Alan Silverwood |
| CB | Craft Bitz |
| EA | Edable Art |
| GI | Great Impressions |
| FMM | FMM Sugarcraft |
| HP | Holly Products |
| JEM | Jem Cutters c.c. |
| LC | Lindy's Cakes Ltd |
| OP | Orchard products |
| PC | Patchwork Cutters |
| PME | PME Sugarcraft |
| SF | Sugarflair |
| SK | Squire's Kitchen |

# index

abbreviations 136
air bubbles 18
anniversary cakes 42, 50, 118, 126
Artista soft 15, 61
Art Nouveau cakes 42–9, 112–17, 134, 135

ball cakes 124–5, 126–31
balls, piping 56, 62, 122
ball tins 6, 7, 8, 11
ball tools 6, 7
beads 26–7
birthday cakes 42, 50, 58, 64, 72, 84, 104, 118, 126
bonfire night 118
bon voyage 78
brushes 6, 7
buttercream 15

cake boards 6, 7
    covering 17, 18
carving cakes 4, 16, 19–20
chocolate cake 8, 9
christening bricks cake 84–9, 133
Christmas cakes 58–63, 126–31
cocktail stick 6, 7
colour 24–5, 40–1, 61
conical cakes 104–11
covering cakes 16–18, 21
craft knife 6, 7
cut-outs 40–1, 78, 112
cutters 5, 6, 7, 40
cutting cakes 12, 33
cutting wheel 6, 7

dowels 6, 7, 22
Dresden tool 6, 7

embossers 6, 7, 49, 53, 88, 108
engagement cakes 42, 118
equipment 6–7

fat, white vegetable 15
fillings 15, 16
fish, sparkling mosaic cake 112–17
flavourings 8
flower paste 15, 42, 118
flowers
    Art Nouveau lilies 42–9, 134, 135
    beaded 34–5
    eastern ornament cake 101
    falling leaf cake 104–11, 134
    funky cake 72–7
    Op Art boxes 90–5
    orchid cake 118–25, 132

pastel tower cake 36–41
fluting tool 6, 7
foam pad 6, 7
freezing cakes 16, 19
fruit cake 10–11

gardeners 64
geometric shapes 64, 77, 81–3, 90–5, 97
gilding 47, 70–1, 83, 131
glazes 14, 16, 70
Greek inspirations cake 78–83, 132

hexagonal cake 96

icing
    coloured 24–5
    royal 15
    sugarpaste 14, 18, 21
icing sugar 17
Indian-style cake 96–103, 134

jewellery
    basics 26–7
    cake decorations 30–5, 41, 54–7, 64–71, 96–103, 118–25, 126–31, 134

large cakes 12
leaf-shaped decoration 104–11, 134
levelling cakes 8, 16
lighting 25
lining tins 7

Madeira cake 8, 9
marbled paste 122–3
marzipan 16–17
measurements 6
mini-cakes 13
modelling paste 14, 24, 39, 48, 64–71
mosaic design 112–17
Mother's Day 118
moulds 6, 7, 107
multi-ribbon cutter 6, 7
musical cake 50–7, 133

oasis fix 6, 7
Op Art boxes 90–5

painting cakes 25, 69, 110, 122, 128
paint palette 6, 7
paisley decorations 96, 100–3
palette knife 6, 7
pastillage 14, 57, 61, 129
pins 6, 7
piping bag/tubes 6, 7
portions 12

posy pick 6, 7
preparation/planning 5
puzzles 64

quilting tool 6, 7

recipes 8–11, 12
relief shapes 64–71, 88
retirement cake 64, 104
retro style 42, 90–5, 104, 112, 134
rolling pin 6, 7

scissors 6, 7
scriber 6, 7, 46, 76, 107, 109
separators 22, 23, 96, 118
set square 6, 7, 67
size of cake 12
smoother 6, 7
snowflake cake 58–63
spacers 6, 7, 18
spirit level 6, 7
spoons, measuring 6, 7
stacking cakes 22–3
storing cakes 16, 23
sugar glue 14
sugarpaste 14, 18, 21, 24–5
sugar shaper 6, 7
suppliers 5, 136
swimmers 112

tiered cakes 12, 22–3
tins 6, 7, 13
tools 6, 7, 26

wedding cakes
    Art Nouveau lilies 42–9, 134, 135
    cosmic ball 126
    eastern ornament 96–103, 134
    falling leaf 104–11
    funky flowers 72–7
    ice-blue jewels 30–5
    Op Art boxes 90
    orchid 118–25, 132
    perfect harmony 50–7, 133
    simply spectacular 41
    snowflake 58–63
    sparkling fish 112–17
wine enthusiast 64–71, 133
wire ornaments 26, 113, 115, 126–31
wonky cakes 4
    carving 19–20
    covering 21
    dowelling 22
    funky flowers 72–7
    pastel flower tower 36–41
    sparkling fish 112–17
work board 6, 7

**Lindy Smith** is a highly experienced cake designer and author of six other cake-decorating books. Other books by Lindy for David & Charles are *Creative Celebration Cakes*, *Storybook Cakes*, *Celebrate with a Cake!* and *Party Animals*.

Lindy runs a highly successful cake design company called Lindy's Inspirational Cakes, which produces unusual and innovative, highly personalised wedding cakes as well as providing a mail-order service and on-line shop for sugarcraft equipment, cake jewellery supplies and cake separators. Her gorgeous wedding cakes are frequently featured in wedding magazines – see her website for a taster of the diversity of her creativity, from stylish and sophisticated cakes to fun and light-hearted creations.

As an accredited demonstrator of the British Sugarcraft Guild, Lindy travels widely, sharing her extensive knowledge with fellow sugarcrafters, and her trade stand can usually be found at most of the major UK sugarcraft shows. Lindy also appeared on the television programme *Xchange* for CBBC in 2006 and previously appeared in *The Generation Game* and a sugarcraft series on *Good Food Live*.

For more details please visit Lindy's website: www.lindyscakes.co.uk.